AGE OF VIKRAMĀDITYA

AGE OF VIKRAMĀDITYA

(From the First Century B.C. to the Second Century A.D.)

Dr. K.C. Jain
Ph.D., D.Litt
Dr. P.C. Jain
Ph.D.

AGAM KALA PRAKASHAN
DELHI-110052

First Published : 2009

ISBN : 978-81-7320-086-1

Published by :
Dr. Agam Prasad, M.A., Ph.D., Diploma in Museology
for **Agam Kala Prakashan**
34, Central Market, Ashok Vihar,
Delhi-110052
Ph. : 27212195, 47098550, 65688806-7
Fax : 91-11-27212195
Email: agambooks@gmail.com, agambook@yahoo.com

Laser Typesetting by :
Elegant Printographics
319, IIIrd Floor, R.G. Complex-I,
Sector-14, Rohini, Delhi-85.

Printed at :
Chawla Offset
Delhi - 110052

Printed in INDIA

Preface

Vikramāditya was one of the greatest rulers of the world but his greatness has been ignored by historians.

This work of Vikramāditya was taken because it was of great importance and it was interpreted wrongly. In our opinion no one can stand in comparison with this wonderful personality. It was not a myth but reality. Some scholars have tried to prove his historicity.

In chapter 1, the origin, settlement and migration of the Mālavās have been discussed, but there are differnt views among the scholars.

In chapter 2, the sources – archaeology, literature and writings of the foreigners have been discussed. In archaeology, we have discussed the excavations and exploration of the histroical sites, and the antiquities. As a result, the inscriptions, coins etc. found have been used for the purpose of history. Literary works also prove to be useful directly and indirectly for the history of Vikramāditya. There is a gap of three hundred years for preparing the history. Now, it has disappeared. Vikramāditya always showed unassuming character. Scholars have been trying to build-up the history of Vikramāditya from different angles.

The writings of the foreigners were utilised for the purpose of history. Co-relatiòn of different sources for reconstructing history has been attempted.

In chapter 3, there is ancestory and early career of Vikramāditya. He got early training from his parents. He got education in different branches of learning from Sānḍīpani and *Kālakāchārya* at Ujjain.

In chapter 4, Vikramāditya and his era have been discussed. As *Vikraṁa Samvata* is historical, we should not doubt about Vikramāditya as a historical figure.

In chapter 5, Historicity of Vikramāditya has been discussed. After examining the different views, we come to the conclusion that Vikramāditya was the historical figure who also founded the *Vikrama Saṁvata* in the 57 B.C.

In chapter 6, the comparitive study of Vikramāditya in history has been discussed.It has been pointed out that great people were born for removing the sufferings of the people.

In chapter 7, conquests and extent of empire of Vikramāditya has been discussed. In order to get an idea of extent of empire, corroborative evidence from different sources has been attempted.

In chapter 8, it included the tribal states of Monarchial, and Republics and Wild Tribes Punjab, Rajasthan, Malwa and Gujarat. There were cordial relations among these states.

In chapter 9, the administration of Vikramāditya has been discussed. Territorial-divisions, Official-divisions and revenues have been explained. It has been pointed out, how the *Kṣhatrapa* system came into existence with the contact of Kuṣhāṇas. The republics of India were of political importance, and tribal states have been also taken into account. The administration of *Khāraveḷa* and Rudradāmana is also of significance.

In chapter 10, Vedic religion has been described. Besides, some new Brahmanical religions such as Śaivism, Vaiṣṇavism came into existence. Buddhism first developed greatly as known from the monuments, but soon dispppeared forever. It has been discussed how Jainism developed highly by the efforts of Jaina scholars and monks. Emphasis was laid on penances.

In chapter 11, it is devoted to the social conditions. Vikramāditya was a far sighted person and brought social changes created by new circumstances. Old caste disappeared and new castes were formed. Foreigners like Yavanas, Śakas and Kuṣāṇas etc. were merged into Brāhamaṇa Hindu society. New social works were written to meet social changes. Inter-caste marriages also started at this time. Food and drink habits also changed. Wild tribes were converted into new castes.

In chapter 12, economic conditions changes have been described. The kingdom of Vikramāditya became rich. A large number of coins of different types were discovered. Merchants occupied important position because of their wealth. There was also increase in agricultural production, and mines were discovered.

In chapter 13, art and architecture has been described critically. Because of the loss of time and place, most of the characteristics of art disappeared. Those which are in existence, give an idea of art and architecture. The monuments of Sāñchī give us an idea of features of the Buddhist pillars, *stūpa* and monastry and temple. Beside we know about Vaiṣṇava pillar of Nagori.

In chapter 14, education, literature and sciences have been described. During this period, Ujjain became the most important seat of learning in education, literature and sciences. Because of the development in all spheres, it seems that rays of light radiated all around.

In chapter 15, Vikramāditya and his subjects have been discussed.

In chapter 16, Conclusion, Golden Age of Vikramāditya has been explained.

Ujjain

Kailash Chand Jain
Prakash Jain

Contents

Abbreviations

1. ABORI	:	Annals of the Bhandarkar Oriental Research Institute, Poona
2. ACTR	:	Ancient Cities and Towns of Rajasthan
3. ASC	:	Archaeological Survey of India Reports by Alexander Cunningham.
4. ASI	:	Archaeological Survey of India Annual Reports.
5. BHSJCIC	:	A Brief Historical Survey of Jainism and its contribution to Indian Culture.
6. CCIM	:	Catalogue of the Coins in the Indian Museum by V.A. Smith, Calcutta
7. CII	:	Corpus Inscription Indicorum
8. EI	:	Epigraphia Indica
9. EBCTDRAREBJ	:	P. Earliest Buddhist Circular temple by Dayaram Sahani

		Report of Archaeological Remains and excavations at Bairath, Jaipur
10. RARER	:	Report of Archaeological remains and Excavations at Rairh.
11. IAR	:	Indian Archaeology, A Review
12. IHQ	:	Indian Historical Quaterly
13. JNSI	:	Journal of the Numismatic Society of India.
14. JRAS	:	Journal of the Royal Asiatic Society of Great Britain and Ireland, London.
15. KHT	:	Kālidāsa and his Times.
16. MTA	:	Malwa through the Ages.
17. NS	:	Numismatic Supplement.
18. PHAI	:	Political History of Ancient India.
19. SBI	:	Select Inscriptions bearing on Indian History and Civilization.
20. V.U.	:	Vikramāditya of Ujjaiyīni.

List of Plates

Chapter 1

Physical Features of Malwa and its Cultural Influence

Introduction

Vikramāditya the great ruler, flourished from the first century B.C. to the second century A.D. The territory of this kingdom included the Mālavā region, and some other ancient territories. Among the territorial units of Vikramāditya, Mālavā republic is the oldest.The physical features of Mālavā described below are noteworthy. These territioral regions also influnced the history of Vikramāditya's kingdom. The territorial regions, in the neighbourhood have been used for historical purpose. These physical features of the kingdom also served the cultural purpose. The capital of this kingdom remained Ujjain.

Origin of the Name

Both the names Mālavā and Mālaya are known from literary, epigraphical and numismatic sources.

R.D. Douglas[1] assumes that Mālaya is the older form of the tribal name, but nothing can be stated definitely.

There is a controversy among scholars about the origin of the name *Māla*, occuring on some coins, which is regarded by R.D. Douglas[2] as the name of a king, the founder of the tribe; but it appears to have been intended for Mālaya or Mālavā. A.C. Carelleyle[3] and Vincent Smith[4], on the basis of the peculiar legends on some coins, hold that these are the names of foreign rulers. It may be concluded from this that the Mālavās were foreigners. But J. Allan[5] rightly points out thay they are too late for the Śakas and too early for the Hūṇas. These names do not bear any resemblance to any Śaka or Hūṇa name. D.C. Sircar[6] suggests that the name of Mālavā, like that of the Mālaya mountain range, is probably derived from the Dravidian word '*Malai*', meaning hill. Thus originally, it meant a Dravidian hill tribe. This is based on speculation because there is no concrete evidence of the existence of a hill tribe of this name in the south.

Raj Bali Pandey[8] suggests the the Mālavās branched off from the Malla people of the famous *Mallarāṣṭra* situated in the Gorakhpur Division of Uttara Pradesh. The first derivative from '*Mallas*' was Mālayā, or Malāya, which subsequently became Mālavā. The *Mallas* were the descendents of Ikṣvāku of the Solar race. According to the *Vālmīkī Rāmāyaṇa*, the epithet of Candraketu, the son of Lakṣmaṇa, was Malla, and he founded the *Mallarāṣṭra* and his descendents were called Mallas. The Solar race of the *Mallas* is also proved by Buddhist literature.[8] From the Nāndasā inscription[9] of 226 A.D., it is known that they were as famous as the Ikṣvākus. But the identification of the Mālavās with Malla does not seem to be reasonable.

On the basis of the peculiar legends of the coins, Kalyan Kumara Das Gupta[10] is of the view that these Mālavās were probably non-Aryan. These are not meaningless attempts to reproduce parts of '*Mālavānām-jayaḥ*', but they mention the names of the Mālavās chiefs who belonged to the non-Āryan stock.There is at least one coin in the Indian Museum which definitely bears the name of the tribe Mālavā, together with one with the curious expression 'MAJUPA'[11]. '*Majupa*' seems to be a Mālavā chief who was a non-Āryan. Words of non-sanskrit origin, like the present legends, are not altogether absent in Indian Numismatics. Words like *Ralimasa, Dojaka* and *Atakataka* appear on a group of *Negama* coins found at Taxila[12]. Scholars regard them as proper names, either of persons, or of places.[13] On this analogy, the outlandish words on Mālavā coins may be regarded as proper names, and they seem to be the names of Mālavā chiefs probably of non-Āryan origin. J. Allan[14] thinks that these are not personal names, as they are without any normal genitive suffix. Against this, it may be pointed out, that even the Nāga coinage, to which some of the Mālavā coins are closely related, has no use of a genitive sign[15]. Hence, these legends on the Mālavā coins seem to be the personal names of the Mālavā, and they probably lived in the third or fourth century A.D.

Some of the classical writers furnish interesting details about their physiognomy. One of them says that they were of great stature and were amongst the tallest *men* in Asia. Their complexion was black, and they were very simple in their habits.[16] The *Viṣṇudharmottaram,*[17] describing a Mālavā of 104 *āṅgulas* in measure, observes that he is dark like the *mudga* pulse, with a very beautiful body, with a slender waist and arms reaching the knees. From the account of both these sources regarding their complexion, it may be inferred that they were not Āryans. But from the legends of the coins which belong to the third or fourth century A.D., and the account of the classical writers and the literary sources, no conclusion can be drawn regarding their origin. We do not find such names of the Mālavās in the Nāndsā inscription.

The earliest evidence of the existence of the Mālavā in the fourth century B.C. in the Punjab is found in the works of Greek classical writers who mention them as *Malloi.* It seems that like many other tribes of ancient India, the Mālavā had their original home in the Punjab; from there they spread in different directions and formed settlements.

Movements and Settlements of the Mālavās

The Mālavā were numerous in Ancient India. It seems that they had separate settlements in the Punjab, Rajasthan, Malwa, etc. As early as the time of the *Mahābhārata,* a two or three fold classification of the Mālavās were known, *viz.* the Mālavās of the East, North and West[18]. According to E.J. Thomas[19], the Mālavās of the Jaina *Bhagavāti Sūtra* could not have been in the Punjab, but must have been located in Central India.

From later literary sources, it is known that the Mālavās were ruling over Mālavā in the first century B.C. From epigraphical and numismatic sources, it seems that the Mālavās continued to flourish in south-east Rajasthan from the second century B.C. to the fourth century A.D. D.R. Bhandarkar[20] and other scholars believe that there were three main stages in the movement and settlement of the Mālavās. First, they were in the Punjab; in the second stage they were in the south-east Rajasthan, and in the third they moved south-wards and settled in the north-western part of Madhya Pradesh, known as Mālavā.

Mālavās in the Punjab

We know about the Mālavā of the Punjab from the classical writers, early Sanskrit Grammarians and the epics. The Greek writers, who wrote on Alexander's Indian campaign, mentioned the *Malloi* together with Oxydrakoi. These may be identified with the Mālavā and the *Kṣūdrakas* respectively. Both formed a confederation which heroically opposed Alexender. According to Arrian,[21] they were the most numerous and warlike of the Indians in those regions of the country. Arrian[22] calls the *Malloi* a race of independent Indians. Alexander very narrowly escaped in his war with the Mālavā-*Kṣūdrakas* confederacy. The confederate army consisted of 90,000 foot-soldiers, 10,000 cavalry and 900 war chariots. The Macedonians lost heart at the prospect of meeting army. However, they were defeated, but they survived and sent hundred ambassdors to Alexender.

There is a difference of opinion among scholars about the location of the Mālavā in the Punjab. V.A. Smith[23] believes that the *Malloi* occupied the country below the confluence of the Hydaspes (Jhelum) and Akesines (Chenab), *i.e.* the country comprising the Jhang District, and the whole, or greater portion, of the Montgomery District. But Mc Crindile[24] thinks that the territory of the Mālavās was to a great extent, comprising a part of the modern Doab formed by the Akesines and the Hydraotes, and extending, according to Arrian, to the confluence of the Akesines and the Indus. That is, the modern Multan District with parts of the Montgomery District. H.C. Ray Chaudhuri[25] places them in the valley of the lower Hydraotes 'north of the confluence of the river and the Chinab.' Their capital was on Ravi, which is identified by A. Cunningham[26], with Multan.

Early Sanskrit Grammarians also refer to the Mālavā people. Pāṇini,[27] while illustrating the '*Ayudha-Jīvī-Saṁgha*' (the republican people living on the profession of arms), showed the Mālavā *Kṣūdrakas*. The Kāśikā[28] commentary on the *Aṣṭādhyāyi* of Pāṇini, clearly states that the Mālavā and the *Kṣūdrakas* were most prominent among the Āyudhajīvī-Saṁgha. While commenting on one of the *Sūtras* of Pāṇini, Pātañjalī[29] refers to the *Kṣūdrakas* and the Mālavā together, in the instance of the Kṣartiya Janapadas.

In the *Mahābhārata*, in one place, they are mentioned with Trigartas,[30] and in another place, they are referred to with the *Śibis* and *Ambaṣṭhas*[31]. From the *Mahābhārata*, it is known that the Mālavās were related to the Mādras who occupied the territories round about Sialkot. From the context, it appears that *Mālavas* were surrounded by the Trigartas and Mādras in the north-east Punjab, and *Ambaṣṭhas* and the *Śibis* in the north of Sind. They occupied a great part of the Southern Punjab, including the districts of Firozpur and Ludhiana, and the former states of Jind, Patiala, Nabha, and Maler Kotla which is still called Mālavā.[32] During *Mahābhārata* war, they fought on side of the Kauravas.

Mālavās of Rajasthan

Because of the Indo-Greek invasions, the Mālavās, or at least a large section of the tribe, like other tribes under the pressure, migrated to Rajasthan and other parts of India, and this migration seems to have continued down to the Scythian conquest of India. The occupation of the south-east Rajasthan by the Mālavās from the second century B.C. to the fourth century A.D. is known from both the numismatic and epigraphical evidences . In south-east Rajasthan, the capital of the Mālavā republic was Mālavānagara,[33] which has been identified with the modern Nagar.

More than 6,000 Mālavās coins were discovered at Nagar. There is a controversy among scholars about the dates and the legends. A.C. Carlleyle[34] and A. Cunningham[35] assigned the *Mālava* coins to the period between 250 B.C. and 250 A.D. or 350 A.D. as the latest. But to V.A. Smith[36] and B.J. Rapsion[37] the intial date is not earlier than 150 B.C., and these coins continued up to the fourth and fifth centuries A.D. Raj Bali Pandey[38] thinks that these coins were issued by Vikramāditya in order to commemorate his victories against the Śakas in the first centuries B.C. J. Allan[39] seems to be right in assigning these coins to the period between the second century A.D. and the early part of the fourth century. These Mālavā coins may be divided into three groups.

The first group bears the legends, "*Mālavānām Jayaḥ*" or "*Mālavā Ganasya Jayaḥ*". The coins have the vase, lion, bull, king's head, fan-tail-peacock and other objects, as their reverse design. The two other groups of coins are ascribed to the Mālavās primarily because they were found along with the Mālavā coins, and resembled the latter in fabric. The coins of the second group do not bear any legend, while those of the third category have meaningless legends in which the name of the Mālavās cannot usually be traced.

V.A. Smith[40] regarded these coins as the most curious and enigmatical in the vast range of Indian coinage. This is partly due to the meaningless legends on the third class of the coins, and partly also to the light weight and small size of many coins. V.A. Smith suggested that these peculiar legends on the latter group are the names of certain foreign rulers who issued them. J. Allan[41] thinks that they are not names but, in most cases, meaningless attempts to reproduce parts of "*Mālavāṇām Jayaḥ.*" D.C. Sircar[42] does not regard these coins as the geniune monetary issues of the Mālavās but they were minted by the local goldsmiths in imitation of the Mālavā coins in order to meet the needs of the people. Kalyan Kumar Das Gupta[43] is of the view that these coins were of the

Mālavā chiefs who belonged to non-Āryan stock.

In Rajasthan and Malwa, the Mālavās were gradually divided into sections and groups known as *Sogin, Maukhari, Gardabhilla,* etc. ruling over different areas. They carried on a constant and tireless struggle against the Śakas. They also brought about the revival of the Vedic religion by performing different kinds of sacrifices.

In the begining of the second century A.D., these Mālavās are known to have fought with their neighbours, the *Uttamabhadras* of the Ajmer region, as well as the latter's allies of the *Kṣaharāta Śakas* of Western India. From the Nasik inscription of Uṣavadāta[1], it appears that Uṣavadāta, the son-in-law of Nahapana inflicted a crushing defeat upon the Mālavās. But the Mālavās soon recovered their position. From the Nāndasā inscription, it is known that a Mālavā leader of the Sogin clan, whose name has been read as "Śrīsoma" by A.S. Altekar,[45] and as 'Nandisoma' by M. Venkataramayya,[46] raised the standard of revolt and celebrated in 225 A.D. the *Ekaṣaṣṭirāṭīra* sacrifice to proclaim the independence of his republic. Curiously, this record does not mention the names of the enemies defeated, but is is possible they may have been the Western Kṣatrapas. This ruler was the son of Jayasoma, grandson of Bhṛguvardhana, and great-grandson of Jayasena. An undated record of Nāndasā mentions *Mahāsenāpati* Bhaṭṭisoma. In the Nāndasā inscription, there is mention of "*Mālavāgaṇa viṣaya*", which according to A.S. Altekar, extended over a considerable portion of south-eastern Rajasthan, comprising parts of the states of Udaipur, Jaipur, Tonk and Ajmer. A fragmentary record[47] dated K.E. 284 (227 A.D.) from Barnal, mentions a ruler whose name ended in the word '*Vardhana*' it is possible that he also belonged to some clan of the *Mālavās.*

It seems that the Maukharīsa of Badwa in the Kota District were branch of the Mālavā. From the Badwa stone pillar inscription[48], it is known that the Maukharīsa performed a *trirātra* sacrifice in 239 A.D., The Allahabad pillar inscription[49] also speaks of the Mālavā, together with the tribes *Arjunāyanas* and *Yaudheyas.* The question is where the Mālavās were located at this time. The coin legends are similar to those of the *Yaudheyas* and the *Arjunāyanas.* The places of their inscriptions, at Nāndasā, Badwa and Barnal, and their coins, indicate that they were living in south-east Rajasthan.

Mālavās in Avanti

That the *Gardabhillas* were a branch of a wider community of the Mālavās is known from a Jaina work, the *Vicāraśreṇī* of Merutuṅgācārya of the fourteen century. It is said that they ruled over Ujjain for 135 years. They were dislodged from Avanti by the invasion of the Śakas, but their leader, Vikramāditya, inflicted a crushing defeat on them in 57 B.C. In order to commemorate his victory, he decided to inaugurate a new era.

From the beginning of the fifth century A.D., the Mālavās seem to have settled around Mandsor. The Mandsor stone inscription[50] of 436 A.D. is, perhaps the first inscription in Malwa proper dated in the Mālavā *Saṁvata* 493. This Mālavā era commenced in 57-58 B.C.

and was traditionally discovered by the Mālavagaṇa. The Aulikaras, who began to rule with a capital at Daśapura, from around the fourth century A.D., were probably a clan of the Mālavās.

These Aulikars seem to be responsible for the name. Mālavā being applied to the territory from about the fifth century A.D. From the Balághat plates[51] of Pṛthvīsena II, it is known that Vākāṭaka king Narendrasena, established his suzerainty over the lords of Kośala, Mekala and Mālavā. Here, Mālavā together with Kośala and Mekala, has been used in the sense of territory probably around Mandsor. The contemporary ruler of Mālavā at that time seems to be the Aulikara ruler, who had his capital at Daśapura.

In early times, the Mālavā and the Avanti were different territorial names, as known from literary sources, but in later times, the territory of Avanti seems to have been designated the name of the Mālavā. The earlier works, such as the *Kāmasūtra*[52] of Vātsyāna, refers to Avanti and Mālavā separately, Bharata in his *Nāṭyaśāstra,*[53] which belongs to about the same period as the *Kāmasūtra,* characterises the people of Avanti, Saurāṣṭra and Mālavā as having the same style. For the first time in the fifth century A.D., the Mālavās, in the territorial sense, denoted Western Mālavā where the Aulikaras, a branch of the Mālavās, ruled, and where the Mālavā era was current. The Eastern Mālavā was under the possession of the Guptas who introduced Gupta era there.

Mālavā Kingdom

From about the first century B.C., the region was known from the name Mālavā *Janapada*, and this name continued to the present. The name of Uniyara near Jaipur, proves that it assumed the teritorial name *Mālava* This ancient name Mālavā Nagar continued up till the tenth century A.D.

From the above, it seems that the territory of Vikramāditya included Western Malwa and Eastern Rajasthan. Malwa is concerned with the names of the other territories.

In the Dholpur inscription[54] of the ninth century A.D., the name of the *Saṁvat* Vikramāditya has been used for the first time.

When Prabhākaravardhana is called an axe to the Mālavā glory[55], Kumāragupta and Mādhavagupta are called the sons of the Mālavā king[56], the murderer of Grahavarman is called the wicked Lord of Mālavā[57], and Rājyavardhana resolves to uproot the Mālavā[58]. In all these different cases, Bāṇa must always have meant it in the sense of some geographical or political entity. Even in his *Kādambarī*, there is a reference to both Avanti and *Mālava*. In the commentary of the *Kāmasūṭra* of Vātsyāyana, we are told that Ujjaiyinī denoted Western Malwa and where Mālavā only is mentioned, it should be taken to mean Eastern Malwa.[59] Relying on these sources scholars generally believe that in the seventh century A.D., Malwa was comprised of Eastern Malwa. R.S. Tripathi observes, "It may not be unreasonable to suggest that Mahāsenagupta, son of Dāmodaragupta, retired to some part of Malwa which was probably Eastern Malwa corresponding to the Bhilsa District on the Vetravati. H.C. Rayachauduri[61] remarks that Mahāsenagupta was probably the king of Malwa (Mālavā) possibly Eastern Malwa. According to B.C. Law[62] it is difficult to identify the Mālavā kingdom of Mahāsenagupta and Devagupta but it is probably identical with Pūrva Mālavā, that lay between Prayāga and Bhilsa.

D.C. Sircar[63] also holds that the application of the name Mālavā to Avanti or the Ujjaiyinī region, does not seem to have been popular before the Paramāra occupation of that area in the latter half of the tenth century A.D. This does not seem to be correct. There are proofs that even in the seventh century A.D., Avanti with Ujjaiyanī, was called Mālavā. In the *Kādambarī*, Bāṇa mentions Ujjain on the Śiprā river, and he also refers to the women of Malwa (Mālavī) associated with Ujjain in such a way, that there is hardly any doubt that the women of Ujjain were known as *Mālavīs* or women of Mālavā in his time. This makes it clear that Mālavā of Bāṇa included Ujjain. Bāṇa mentions the beautiful women of Mālavā (Mālavī) in the *Harṣacarita*, when Harṣa inspects the spoils of victory won by his brother from the king of Mālavā[64]. We have already seen that Mālavī (or women of *Mālavā*) are associated with Ujjain, and therefore, it is reasonable to hold that *Mālavīs* of *Harṣhacarita* also must have included the women of Ujjain. In the Aihol inscription,[65] the Lāṭas, Mālavās and *Gurjaras*, have been described as feudatories of Pulukeśin II. The name Avanti continued for the Ujjaiyinī region even when the name

Mālavā became popular. We cannot conclude from these names that they were separate regions.

Mo-La-P'O of Yuanchwang

The Chinese pilgrim Yuan Chwang[66] mentions *'Mo-la-p'o'* country, which was situated near the river Mahi (Chinese *Moha*) in Gujarat and comprised Kheta (modern Kaira) and Ānandapura (modern Vadnagar). This territory was ruled by Śilāditya of the Maitraka dynasty of Valabhi. He distinguishes it from the country 'Wu-she-yanna' (Ujjain). He seems to have been confused in taking the provincial seat as a separate principality. At this time, Molap'o, with Ujjain, was governed by the ruler of Maitraka dynasty.

The 'Mo-la-p'o' of Yuan Chwang may be identified with *Mālavāka Viṣaya* or *Bhukti* mentioned in the two inscriptions[67] of Dhruvasena II, dated 320 and 322 (639-40, 640-641 A.D.). These grants prove that there was a Mālavāka province of the Valabhi kingdom. The first inscription records that the king made a grant on the eastern boundary of Navagrāmaka, in the *Bhukti* of Mālavāka, whereas the second inscription refers to his grant of land on the southern boundary of Candraputraka in the *Bhukti* of Mālavāka. Navagrāmaka mentioned in the copper plate grant, has been identified with Nogawa in the Ratlam District. Nogawa is actually situated on the Malwa Plateau. This Mālavāka province of Valabhi might have extended so far as Ujjain which is only 58 km from Nogawa. It is suggested that a branch of the *Mālavās* might have settled in north and eastern

Gujarat, where Yuan Chwang found them, and he therefore called the country 'Mo-la-p'o'. It is possible that the Valabhi kingdom had a province which included a portion of Mālavā, and hence it was called 'Mālavāka'.

In the post Gupta period, the Mālavās seem to have gone eastward also. Some copper plates of Pāla kings refer to the *Kulikas* or cultivators, as consisting not only of the Khasas and Hūṇas, but also of the Mālavās.[68] Their expansion is attested by a late inscription[69] which states that *Dandanāyaka* Anantapāla, a feudatory of Chālukya Vikramāditya VI, subdued the *Sapta* Mālavā countries up to the Himālayas[70], marking the last known state in the movement of the tribe.

Contributions

The contributions of the Mālavās to Indian culture are remarkable. Originally, they were *Āyudhajivā Saṁgha.* They were essentially an army, because they all adopted the profession of war. They provided heroic resistance against Alexander the Great and afterwards, they continued their fight against the Śakas and Kuṣāṇas for the protection of the freedom of the country. They established strong republican traditions. On their coins, we find the mention of *Mālavāgaṇa* but not the names of their rulers. By the third century A.D., they had gradually assumed a monarchical constitution, as we find hereditary rulers mentioned in the Nāndasā inscription. But they still maintained the republican traditions in that they did not assume that the title of *Rājā* and *Mahārājā*, but of *Senāpati*. This shows that their state was still primarily a military one.

This Mālavā republic revived the Vedic religion by erecting *yūpas* (sacrifical pillars) and performing different sacrifices. From 58 B.C., a new era was recorded which was first known as Kṛita, then Mālavā and afterwards *Vikrama Saṁvat.* It has been mentioned in one inscription[71] that it has been traditionally handed down by the Mālavā republic.

Importance of Mālavā Tribe

The importance of the Mālavā tribe is emphasised by the fact that it has been mentioned in the *Viṣṇudharmottaram*[72] and the *Bṛihatsaṁhitā.*[73] These works divide the people into five main groupings – Haṁsa, Bhandra, Mālavya, Ruchaka and Śaśaka for purposes of their representation in art and furnish details about the physical peculiarities of each of these types. The territorial units, castes and dialects, were named after the Mālavās. Even today, a large part of the Southern Punjab, comprising the districts of Firozpur and Ludhiana, and the old states of Jind, Patiala, Nabha and Malerkotla, is known as Malwa. The dialect used in the region extending from Firozpur to Bhatinda is known as Malawai. The territory connected with the plateau in Madhya Pradesh has been called Mālavā since the first century B.C. The name Mālavā has also survived in Brāhmaṇa community, known as *Mālavīs.*

It seems that from the seventh century A.D., the *Mālavas* settled in one particular region which became known as Malwa. Both historically and traditionally, Malwa comprises the whole of Western Madhya Pradesh, the Vindhyas in the south, Sagar-Damoh plateau and Bundelkhand in the east,. Guna-Shivpuri region and Rajasthan in the north, and Gujarat and Aravallis in the west. The limits are 21^0 50' N and 24^0 30' N and 74^0 30' E- 87^0 81'E, covering an area of about 47,760 square km. At present, this region included eleven western Districts of Madhya Pradesh – Indore, Ujjain, Dewas, Dhar, Mandsor, Ratlam, Rajgarh, Shajapur, Sehore, Vidisha and Raisen. These limits are correct since all the ancient kingdoms of Malwa-Kuntel (Mandsor), Bagar (Ratlam), Rath (Dhar), Sondwara(Mahidpur), Unaiwara (Rajgarh) and Khichiwara (Raisen) are included within these boundaries.

THE GEOGRAPHICAL BACKGROUND

Malwa was one of the most important provinces of India in ancient times, and its influence on Indian culture has been profound Physically, culturally and politically, we may call it the 'Heart of India'. It is the passageway from North India to the Deccan. 'Malwa' implies the plateau region which formed a political unit like 'Magadha' 'Kaliṅga' and 'Saurāṣṭra'. In the sixth century B.C., it became famous under the name of Avanti but from the fifth century onwards it was largely called 'Mālavā'. Malwa covers an area of about 47,760 square km and comprises of the districts of Dhar, Jhabua, Ratlam, Dewas, Indore, Ujjain, Mandsor, Sehore, Shajapur, Raisen and Vidisha[74].

Malwa is drained by three main rivers — the Chambal,

Betwa and Narmada. To the west and north west of this plateau are the *Arāvilli hills*, which is the oldest mountain system on the globe. To the south, it is bounded by the Vindhyas, which are known as mountains but are in fact a series of escarpments overlooking the rift valley of Narmadā. South of the Vindhyas and roughly parallel with them, are the Satpurā mountains. The Vindhyas and Satpurā together form the backbone of middle India. To the north-west of Malwa are the Bundi Hills. The Malwa plateau is buckled on the northern fringes, and Hadauti (Rajasthan) on the west. In fact, the Bundeli, Hadauti and Malwi Cultures coalesce in Vidisha along the Betwa.

This region is largely covered by black soil, which is very fertile for the cultivation of cotton, wheat, sugarcane, groundnuts etc. This black soil was derived from old lava deposits. The area round this region is rich in forests.

This territory of the Malwa region may be divided into the following natural division :

(1) The Central Malwa Plateau,

(2) The North-East Plateau,

(3) The North-West Plateau and

(4) The Narmadā Valley.

The Central Malwa Plateau

Malwa forms a great triangle based onthe Vindhya hills. It is plateau with a mean elevation of 496 m above sea level, interspersed with the Vindhya and Satpurā ranges. It lies between 23° 30' to 24° 30' N and 74° 30' to 78° 10' E. It is terminated on the south by the Great

Vindhya range, on the east by the arm of this same range that strikes north from Bhopal to Chanderi (the *Kulachala Parvata of the purāṇas*), on the west by the branch which reaches from Amjhera to Chittor (in Rajasthan), and on the north by the Mukandwara range which strikes east from Chittor to Chanderi.[75] It consists of the districts of Rajgarh, Shajapur, Dewas, Indore, Ratlam and Dhar.

Physically, it may be described as high tableland, consisting of a gently undulating and inclined plain, which is open and highly cultivated, and which is varied by small conical and table crowned hills, and low ridges. It is watered by numerous rivers and small streams, and favoured with a rich and highly productive soil and a mild climate, conducive to the health and happiness of men.[76]

Physically also, Malwa falls into two different divisions which might, indeed, form separate regions. (i) The Vindhya scarplands of the North, and (ii) the Great Deccan Lava Plateau in the South. There is a great contrast between the Vindhya and the Deccan Lava landscapes. The former is arid and more rugged and harder in appearance.[77]

The river system of Malwa is interesting. This region is watered by several rivers which are led by numerous tributaries, that intersect and irrigate the area in all directions. Among the principal rivers are the Chambal, the Kali Sind, Śiprā, Parbati, Betwa, Mahi and Narmadā. The Chambal, Ken and Betwa rise within 32 km of the Narmadā from the Vindhya escarpments. The Chambal and its tributaries, Kali Sind and a Parbati, have formed a triangluar alluvial basin at about 211-271 m in Kota, above the narrow trough of the lower Chambal, the present site Rana Pratap Sagar Barrage.[78]

Malwa's weather is generally mild, except during the latter part of the year when great and sudden changes often take place. The climate on the whole is pleasant and invigorating.

The North East Plateau

This is narrow outstretch of the great central plateau of Malwa which is made distinctive by the ranges of the Vindhyas encircling it from the east, north and south. With the fertile plateau of Malwa proper easily accessible towards the west, and with its proximity to the fertile Gangetic plains of the east, the region about Vidisha was always prosperous and flourishing, a fact which is amply reflected in the richness of its monuments.[79] In the early times, this region was famous under the name of Daśārṇa.

The North-West Plateau

This comprises of Mandsor and part of the Ratlam District, it is adjacent to Mewar, the land of Rajputs, which is full of hills and sandy tracts. It presents some physical features common to the adjoining region. This tract is hilly and rugged, which aids the development of characteristics required for military way of life, and also, affording facilities for the erection of edifices in stone. The *Mālavās* and the Aulikaras, who ruled over this region, were famous for their heroic deeds. Daśapura (Mandsor) was the famous city of this region.

The Narmadā Valley

The low lying narrow valley of this great river is enclosed by the ranges of the Vindhyas and Satpurā in the north and south respectively. The country is flat and fertile, and cultivation here is more widespread and floursihng. Along the Vindhya hills, the country becomes wilder, and teak forests predominate in this area. The climate, however, is not as mild as that of the plateau in the north. This region was known as *Anupa* in ancient times. On the bank of Narmadā the town of Mahishmati (Maheshwar) once stood, was one of the most ancient cities of India.

These physical features of Malwa have considerably influenced not only the political, but also the cultural history. They have affected the lives and habits of the people, influenced their character and make-up, and invested them with distinctive characterstics. At times the natural beauty of this region inspired poets and writers, like Kālidāsa to write literary works.

In the valleys of the rivers of Narmadā, Chambal, Betwa and others great centres of culture and civilization gradually developed, from the first century B.C. to the second century A.D., specially during the reign of Vikramāditya. In the course of time, the important towns of Ujjain, Maheshwar, Vidiśā, Mandsor, etc., sprang up on the banks of these rivers. Because of the beautiful scenery in the neighbourhood, and the cool breeze, these rivers created a sense of holiness in the minds of the people who, in consequence, used to worship them.

As the climate is good and the soil is fertile in Malwa, most of the people took to agriculture, and other peaceful pursuits such as cottage crafts. There were easy means of livelihood without a hard struggle. The fertile soil and rich resources afforded enough leisure and ease to the people for the development of intellectual pursuits and philosophical speculation, which led to the growth of literature and philosophy. This is one reason for the number of literary giants in this region, who enriched Indian culture by their works. Attracted by the easier way of life, settlers from different parts migrated to this region from time to time.

The facilities of communication led to the development of commerce and trade. As result, this region flourished from the earliest times. The general prosperity is evident from the large numbers of ancient monuments, which are excellent specimens of art and architecture, which have been found in this area.

The strategical importance of Malwa was ever significant. In order to control western India and South India, its occupation was necessary. The Maurya and Gupta rulers conquered it and made it a base for further conquest in this direction. Malwa was always on the crossroads, it also afforded an excellent military base, and its occupation opened the doors for further territorial expansion.

The Śaka Sātavāhana struggle was fought because both the powers wanted to keep this region in their possession.

Thus, historically Malwa displays a curious duality.

The Deccan Lavas provide the only extensive agricultural base in Central India, and so it has retained its individuality; yet as a land of passage, it has constantly changed hands. Its frontiers are least persistent in the North. This is, in part atleast, inherent in the Geography of Malwa compared to that of its neighbouring regions. As it provides by far the best route from Northern India to the Deccan, it has been regarded as a prized possession by all political powers of Northern India and the Deccan.[80]

Such is the stage of Malwa upon which the drama of history and culture was played by Vikramāditya.

REFERENCES

1. *Numismatic supplement*, XXXVII, p.13.
2. *Ibid.*, p. 45.
3. *ASC* VI, p.174.
4. *CCIM*, p.163.
5, *A Catlaogue of the Indian Coins in the British Museum*, p. CVI.
6, *The Age of Imperial Unity*, p.163.
7. *Vikramāditya of Ujjyainī*, p. 78.
8. *The Mahā-parinivvāna-sutta and the Divyāvadāna.*
9. *EI*, XXXVII, p.265.
10. *The Mālvas*, p. 19.
11. *CCIM*, p. 175, no.70 class 2, variety B.
12. A. Cunningham : *Coins of Ancient India*, p. 19; *A Catalogue of the Indian Coins in the British Museum*, p. C XXVI.
13. *Coins of Ancient India*, p. 65; *A Catalogue of the Indian Coins in the British Museum*, p. C XXX.
14. *A Catalogue of the Indian Coins* in the British Museum, p. CVII.

15. *CCIM*, pp. 162, 164; *JRAS*, 1897, p. 643; H.V. Trivedi : *Catalogue of the Coins of the Naga Kings of Padmavati*, 3.
16. McCrindle, *Invasion of Alexender*, p. 85.
17. *Viṣṇudharmottam* III. 85; Kramrisch's Translation, p. 32.
18. *Mbh.* 106-7.
19. *History of Buddhist Thought*, p. 6.
20. *Carmichael Lectures*, pp. 12-13.
21. Arrian *VI*,4.
22. *Ibid.*, *VI*,6.
23. *JRAS*,1903, p. 631.
24. *Invasion of India*, App. note, p. 351.
25. *PHAI*, p. 295.
26. *Ancient Geography of India.*
27. Pāṇini, V, 3.144.
28. *Kāśidlā*, V,3.117.
29. VI,1.68.
30. *Mahābhārata.*
31. *Ibid.*
32. *The imperial Gazetteer*, XVII, p. 105.
33. An inscription dated v.s. 1043 (986A.D.) recently discovered at Nagar calls the place /Māl/avā-nagara and describes its prosperity.
    (Bharata Kaumud l, El, pp. 271-72; EI; XXXIV, p.77).
34. *ASC*, VI, p. 178.
35. *Ibid.*, p. 182.
36. *CCIM*, p. 162.
37. *Indian coins*, p. 15.
38. *Vikramāditya of Ujjaiyinī*, p.39.
39. *A Catalogue of the Indian Coins* in the British Museum, p. C VI.
40. *CCIM*, p. 162.
41. *A Catalogue of the Indian Coins* in the British Museum, p. C VII.

42. *JNSI, XXVI*, pp. 3-4.
43. *The Mālavās*, p.19.
44. *EI*, VIII, p. 78.
45. *Ibid.*, XXVI, p. 265.
46. *IHQ*, XXIX, p. 80.
47. *EI*, XXVI, pp. 118ff.
48. *Ibid.*, XXIII, p. 52.
49. *C II, III*, pp. 6ff.
50. *CII*, III, p. 83.
51. *EI*, IX, pp. 267 ff.
52. *VKS*, p. 370.
53. *Nāṭyaśāstra, XIII*, 29.
54. *V.V.*, p. 4.
55. *HC (CT)*, p. 101, *HC*, Text (parab), p. 120.
56. *Ibid.*, p. 119; Text (*ibid*), p. 138.
57. *Ibid.*, p. 173, *Ibid.*, (Parab), p. 182.
58. (Text Parab), p. 183.
59. *VKS., Adhikaraṇa III.*
60. *History of Kannauj*, p. 46.
61. *PHAI*, p. 512.
62. *Ancient Indian Tribes* II. p. 41.
63. *Ancient Malwa and the Vikramaditya Tradition*, p. 12.
64. Tr Ridding, pp. 47 and 59.
65. *HC Text* p. 227.
66. Yuan-Chwang.
67. *EI*, VII, pp. 188ff.
68. *Abori*, XIII.
69. *EI*, V. p. 229.
70. For these seven *Mālavā* countries, see *PHAI*, p. 582, f.n. 5.
71. *CII*, III, pp. 81 ff.
72. *Viṣṇudharmottaram*, III, 85 *Kramrisch's Translation*, p. 32.
73. Chapter CVIII, *Kern's Tanslation*, *JRAS.* 1875, pp. 93-97.

74. S.D. Misra ; *Natural Regions of the Indian Sub-continent, Type script*, p. 108.
75. *Imperial Gazetteer of India*, XVII, p. 98.
76. *Report on the Province of Malwa and adjoining territories submitted to the Supreme Govt. of British India in* 1822 by John Maccolm.
77. *India and Pakistan*, p. 576.
78. *Ibid.*
79. D.R. Patil: *Cultural Heritage of Madhya Bharat.* p. 5.
80. *India and Pakistan*, p. 576.

Chapter 2

Sources

Introduction

Malwa has a glorious history, and its contribution to the Indian culture is remarkable. Some of the personalities, such as Vikrama and Chastana gained wide fame in India. During the Vikramāditya period, (from the first century B.C. to the second century A.D.), there was all round progress. Sometimes all political and cultural activities centred around Malwa and Malwa's history became that of India. Abundant material found scattered in Malwa throws a flood of light on its past history. The vast material may be broadly divided into three classes: (I)Archaeology, (II) Literature and (III) Writings of foreigners. During this period, we depend on the material obtained from archaeological exploration and excavation, which is limited; but for the subsequent periods of history, the source material gradually becomes richer and richer.

I. ARCHAEOLOGY

Archaeology may be further subdivided into (A) Exploration and Excavation (B) Inscription, (C) Coins, and (D) Monuments.

(A) Exploration and Excavation

The exploration and excavated sites of the age of Vikramāditya such as Ujjain, Maheshwara, Navadatoli, Nagda Manoti, Awara, Earan and Kayatha of Madhya Pradesh and Nagar (*Mālavā Nagar)*, Bairatha, Raidh and Naliyasara of Rajasthan,[1] throw light on the town planning, terracottas, pottery, metal objects, coins, seal etc. on the history of Vikramāditya. The excavation of the above places was important because they are concerned with prosperous condition of the time of *Vikramāditya.* Coins found in the excavation at Raidh mention the name of *Senāpati* but not of the king.[2]

Only the direct sources have been discussed above, but indirect sources have been used whéreever its utilization was felt necessary.

Trial excavations attempted at the historical sites such as Vidīśā, Ujjain, Mandsor and Pawaya, resulted in the discovery of coins, terracottas, sculptures, pottery and other objects which throw a flood of new light on ancient history. *Mālavā nagar* exploration is important source of information throwing light on this aspect.

(B) Inscriptions

A large number of inscriptions have been found in

Malwa, and some of them are very important. They are engraved on rocks, pillars, walls, images, etc. These may broadly be classsified under two groups — (1) those engraved by or on behalf of the ruling authority, and (2) those incised on behalf of private individuals. The second category is found in large number. Generally, they record donations made in favour of religious establishments, or the installation of images for worship. Some times the description is panegyric, and so has to be critically examined before it can be of use.

For the reconstruction of political history, these inscriptions are of great importance. They mention the name of the ruler and his dynasty. Sometimes they give the genealogy of the ruling dynasty. They describe the career and achievements of the rulers. Indirectly, they help us in the location of the kingdom of the ruler, and in determining the extent of his empire. They give a correct picture of the territorial divisions and the offical hierarchy of the different administrations. They inform us about the interstate relations, as also the relations between the suzerain and his feudatories.

The earliest known inscription in Malwa is Aśoka's Sāñchī Pillar Edict[3], which proves that Malwa formed a part of the dominions of the Mauryas. From the Besanagar inscription[4], it is known that Heliodorus was deputed as ambassdor by the Greek king Antialcidas, to the Indian king named Bhāgabhadra Kāśīputra of Vidīśā in the 14th regnal year. The Sātavāhana occupation of Malwa may be proved by a votive inscription[5] found on the southern gateway of the great *stūpa* at Sāñchī, which records a gift of Vāśiṣṭhiputra Ānanda, the foreman of the artisans of Sātakarṇī.

Some inscriptions[6] discovered in Malwa and neighbouring areas throw some light on this problem. At Mandsor, in two inscriptions of Mālavā *saṁvatā* 493 and 589, there occurs a significant expression *Mālavā Gaṇas*. Scholars have interpreted this differently. Kiel-Horn took it in the sense of *Gaṇa* or counting of years. K.P. Jayaswal thinks it an era founded to commemorate the republican constitution. A.S. Altekar translated it as according to the current era in the *Mālavā* republic. The Nandosa Pillar Inscriptions dicloses that the Mālavā *Gaṇa Viṣayā* was using the *Kṛta* era. Thus the *Kṛta*, the *Mālavā* and the Vikrama eras were identical. The era was prevalent in south-east Rajasthan and some portion of Malwa. Though these inscriptions are important, they do not prove positively the existence of Mālavā *Gaṇa* and the Mālavā era, with which he was associated.

The Mālavā tribes were gradually divided in different branches such as Vikrama, Vikramāditya, *Kṛta*, Mālavā, Sogīn, Maukhārī and Aulikara, Girdīabhilla was the father of Vikramāditya who lived in 57 B.C.

The Khāravela inscription is the most important in India, and like Vikramāditya throws light on his conquests and welfare activities as a ruler. Similarly, Kaniṣka was one of the greatest rulers of India, and this fact. throws light on the Jaina antiquities and prosperity during the Kuṣāṇa period.

Chastana was the founder of the Kārdamaka dynasty. Two inscriptions[7] of the Śaka year-II and 72 of

Rudradāmana respectively were discovered at Andhav in Kaccha and Junagarh. Rudradāmana was not only a great conqueror but also administrator.

In Mathurā, a large number of inscriptions of the Kuṣāṇa period have been found. During the reign of the Kuṣāṇa rulers, they are helpful for reconstruction of history. Chaṣṭana was the important ruler of the Śakas. Śaka Sātavāhana coins give an idea of the struggle between Śakas and Sātavāhanas, but it has been mentioned in the *Purāṇas.*

There were mutual relations between Khāravela and Sātakarṇī as known from the antiquities of Mathurā. The same relation existed with Vikarmāditya because both were contemporary. Khāravela had relations with Sātakarṇī. Sātakarṇī had relations with Vikramāditya. This also proves that Khāravela and Vikramāditya were related.

Vikramāditya had relations with Sātavāhanas as known from the Paṭṭāvalries, and Khāravela had relation with Sātakarṇī is mentioned in his inscription.

The material of different types for the history of the kingdom of Vikramāditya is rich in all aspects. Under these circumstances, it is not doubtful to prove the historicity of Vikramāditya.

(C) Coins

Next to inscriptions, coins are the most important source of ancient history. Numerous ancient coins have been discovered at different ancient sites in Malwa. From the study of their symbols, figures, legends, metal and weight, we may reconstruct not only the political, but also the religious and economic history of Malwa.

The earliest known coins are the punch-marked. These punch-marked coins, together with cast coins, have been discovered at Jhalrapatan, Sarangpur, Ujjain, Eran and Maheshwar. This proves that these were old sites. From the study of their symbols, and the layers in which they were discovered in the excavations, it seems that most of them were issued during the Maurya period. Coins of Ujjaiyanī and Eran found in large quantity in Malwa, were issued by the mints of Ujjaiyanī and Eran respectively in the third or second century B.C. when this region was a Maurya province. Some towns such as Ujjain, Eran, Mahiṣamati and Vidīśā, started to issue inscribed coins of their own during this period. This proves the autonomous importance of these towns.

Coins are of much help for the reconstruction of the history of the Śakas, because we have only a few inscriptions and literary works giving reference. The Śakas issued coins which not only gave the name of the ruling king and that of his father, but very often the date in the well known Śaka era as well. This has enabled us to reconstruct the history of the Western Satraps for a period of more than three hundred years. In the Gondarman[8] and the Sarvania *hoards,*[9] the coins of *Mahakshatrapa* Svāmī Rudrasena III are the latest to be represented.

It appears that there was a troublesome period in his reign. The counterstuck coins of Nahapāna issued by Gautamīputra Śātakarṇī, prove that he defeated him and occupied his kingdom. The occupation of some portion of Malwa by the Sātavāhanas is clear from the fact that they issued the peculiar local types of coins in this region. The Nāga coins found in large number at Pawaya and Kutwar are useful for the reconstruction of their history.

That Chandragupta II defeated the Śakas, is clear from the fact that he introduced coins in the imitation of those of the Śakas in the region of Malwa.

The coins are of great help for the history of Vikramāditya. The Ujjain coins with the symbols may be attributed to Vikramāditya. Similarly, the city-coins of Ujjain, Vidīśā and Mahiṣamati are also attributed to the *Mālavā* coins. The coins found at Uniyara[10] with the legend *Mālavā Gaṇa Jaya* are attributed of the Mālavās. Vikramāditya issused them in commemoration of his victory against enemies. There are coins of other republics such as Yaudheya, Arjunāyana and Sibis. There are coins issused by the monorchial states contemporary to Vikramāditya. Among them, the golden coins of Kuṣāṇa and Śaka Sātavahana and Nāga coins are noteworthy. These coins of republics and monorchial states are valuable for the history of the age of Vikramaditya and important facts about him, is that Vikramāditya did not mention his name and place but simply indirectly referred to his symbols.

These coins also throw light on the religious beliefs of the people. Some symbols such as the Sun, bull and elephant found on the punch-marked coins may have some religious and mythological significance. Śiva, represented on some Ujjain coins, symbolically and anthropomorphically, was probably related to *Mahākāla* of Ujjain. From the symbols of bull, *triśūla* and peacock on the coins of the Nāga rulers, it seems that they were followers of Śaivism. On the coins of Viṣṇu, we find the symbols of *chakra*(wheel) and *śaṅkha*(cinch), which may prove his inclination towards Vaiṣṇavism.

The metal and weight of these coins is valuable from the economic point of view. The punch-marked coins found in Malwa are generally of copper; whereas in other regions, they are of silver. They follow the lighter standard of 42 grains of Kośala. The local currency issued from Ujjain and Eran was also of copper. The cross and balls known as Ujjaiyainī-symbol, is perhaps applicable to Ujjain, indicating it as the junction of trade routes. Most of the coins of the Śakas and the Sātavāhanas found in Malwa are of copper and potin. The Nāga rulers issued their coins of the standard of *kākiṇi,* half *kākiṇi* and a quarter *kākiṇi.* The discovery of large number of coins of different periods at Ujjain, Vidīśā and Eran, proves that they were centres of trade and commerce in early times.

(D) Monuments

In addition to inscriptions and coins, we have discovered *stūpas,* monasteries, temples, sculptures, paintings, etc., of Vikramāditya periods. They are of great importance in tracing the history of evolution of Indian art. These artistic pieces furnish invaluable material on the racial types, religious beliefs and superstitions, arms and accountrements, dress and personal ornaments, musical instruments, and several other subjects.

The remains at Sāñchī and in the neighbourhood, from the first century B.C. to the third century A.D., give us an idea of the evolution of art in a particular locality. The monuments and paintings of Bagh are important artistically. That Vaiṣṇavism had a great hold at Vidīśā is clear from the ancient monuments.

II. LITERATURE

Another important source of the ancient Malwa is literature. Though we come across only isolated references to it in literarcy works, they contribute to our research knowledge. Literature may be further classified as follows:

(A) Epic, Purāṇas and Dharma-Śāstras

Only the *Purāṇas* and the epic mention the names of the very old dynasties and kings of Malwa, and the *Vedas* give little information of them. From the *Purāṇas,* we know that the Nāgas and the Haihayas were ruling over this region. As they give mutually confusing and contradictory statements, they cannot be relied upon unless they are confirmed by some independent and contemporary evidence. From the *Purāṇas,* we know that Nāga rulers flourished at Vidīśā, Padmāvatī and Kāntipura. The *Matsyapurāṇa, Narasiṁhapurāṇa. Śivapurāṇa* and *Skandapurāṇa* give description of some holy places like Ujjain. We may call '*Avantikhanda*' of the *Skandapurāṇa,* an ancient guide book of Ujjaiyinī. From the *Mahābhārata,* it is known that Ujjaiyinī became a great seat of learning.

There is a vast material of literary and oral traditions about *Vikramāditya* traced in the lost *Bṛhat-Kathā* composed in *Paiśāchi Prākṛit* by Guṇāḍhya during the reign of Sātavāhana king of Pratiṣṭhāna Guṇāḍhya who may be supposed to have flourished between the first half of the first century B.C. and the commencement of the third century A.D. This time imperial Sātavāhanas ruled Guṇāḍhya describes the great generosity, valour and other qualities of Vikramāditya. The other early allusions to Vikramāditya may be traced from some writers in the *Sattasai of Gāthāsaptasati*[11] as ascribed to Sātavāhana king, named Hāla (Hāla Vāhana or Śālivāhana). The *Gāthāsaptaśatī* alludes to the unbounded generosity of Vikramāditya. Both Guṇāḍhya and Hāla lived close to the time of Vikramāditya. There are some other literary works of the late period such as *Kathā Sarit Sāgara* of Somadeva of Kashmir (1063-89 A.D.), *Virācharita* of Ananta and *Śālivāhana kathā* of Śivadāsa etc. One of the stories about Vikramāditya found in the *Kathā Sarit Sāgara* represents him as the king of Pāṭalīputra and as enemy of the king of Pratiṣṭhāna.

Vikramāditya was highly influenced by the *Arthaśāstra* of Kauṭilya. The works of Kālidāsa, Amarasimgh-Bhāsa and *Dharma-Śāstra* have been used as sources for information for cultural conditions because, they belong to the time of Vikramāditya. The *Kathāsarita Sāgara* and the works of Kālidāsa give the detailed and connected account of the war, conquests and political conditions of Vikramāditya. The *Bṛhatkathā Mañjarīs* contents have sporadic references to the military exploit of Vikramāditya.

(B) Jaina Literature

Jainas have prescribed the traditions of Vikramāditya in many literary works[12] such as Somaprabhas *Kumārapāla Pratibodha* (1184 A.D.), Prabhāchandra's *Prabhāvakacharita* (1127 A.D.), Merutuṅga's *Prabandhachintāmanī* (1304 A.D.), Jina Prabhāsūri's *Vividha tīrthakalpa* (1315 A.D.), Rāja Śekhara's *Prabandhakośa* (1348 A.D.), Devamūrti's *Vikramacharita* (1418 A.D.), Rāmachandra Sūri's *Pañcanḍanḍa Chatra prabandha* (1443 A.D.), *Kālkācārya Kathā* (before 1279 A.D.) and the *Paṭṭāvalīs*. Though these works are of late period, written between the twelfth and fifteeth centuries, they contain many theories which are in the tune with the known facts of history. These works are therefore of value in proving the historicity of Vikramāditya.

Kālkācārya also went to the south and propagated Jainism among the Sātavāhanas as known from the *Kālkācārya Kathānaka.*[13]

The following list of 84 works of Vikramāditya and Kālkācārya also proved their historicity, and also for the propagation of Jainism.[14]

Khāraveḷa summoned the assembly of Jaina scholars for propagation of Jainism in order to edit the several books for Jainas.

According to traditions, Nahapana was defeated at the hands of Gautamīputra, and resigned in 66 A.D. He became Jaina monk and edited the sacred Jaina book after learning from his senior colleague Puṣpadanta and completed Satamkhanḍḍāgama in 75 A.D.[15]

कालकाचार्य सम्बन्धी जैन कथानकों से यह भी ज्ञात होता है कि मालवा क्षेत्र के अनेक नगर एवं ग्राम उस समय जैन धर्म के प्रभाव में थे।

गर्दभिल्ल की मृत्यु के पश्चात् एक जननायक विक्रमादित्य के नेतृत्व में उज्जैन के लोगों ने शकों के विरुद्ध विद्रोह कर दिया। परिणामस्वरूप शकों को उज्जैन से पलायन करना पड़ा।[1] विक्रमादित्य 57 ईस्वी पूर्व में उज्जैन का शासक बना। विक्रमादित्य और विक्रम संवत् भारतीय इतिहास की अनसुलझी पहेलियाँ हैं।[2]

आचार्य कालक विषयक प्राकृत विभाग

1. श्री जिनदासगणि महत्तर विरचित– निषीथ पॅर्ण्यन्तर्गतः कालिकाचार्य कथा संदर्भ सं. 733.
2. श्री संघदास गणि क्षमाश्रमण विरचित –तद्भाष्यन्तर्गत कालिकाचार्य कथा संदर्भ
3. श्री देवचन्द्रसूरि : पूर्णतल्लगच्छ ।
4. मलधारी श्री हेमचन्दसूरि पुष्पमालान्तर्गता कालिकासूरी कथा संवत् 1221
5. श्री भद्रेश्वर सूरि विरचिता – कथावत्यन्तर्गता कालिकाचार्य कथा रचना, संवत् 1221
6. श्री धर्मघोषसूरि विरचिता कालिकाचार्य कथा लेखन संवत् 1473.
7. श्री भावदेवसूरि सं 1312 कालिकाचार्य कथा।
8. श्री धर्मप्रभसूरि सं. 1398 विरचित कालिकाचार्य कथानकम्।
9. श्री विनयन्द्रसूरि कालिकाचार्य कथा।
10. श्री जयानंदसूरि विरचिता कालिकाचार्य कथा।
11. श्री कल्याणतिलक गणि विरचिता बालावषोध कालिकाचार्य कथा।

संस्कृत-गुर्जर विभाग

12. श्री देवेन्द्रसूरि विरचिता कालिकाचार्य कथा, रचना संवत् 13वीं शताब्दी।
13. श्री रामभद्रसूरि विरचिता कालिकाचार्य कथा, रचना संवत् 13वीं शताब्दी।

---

1. पांडेय राजबलि : विक्रमादित्य आफ उज्जयिनी
2. आचार्य कालक एवं विक्रमादित्य विषयक अनेक ग्रन्थ जैन साहित्य में उपलब्ध है। प्रस्तुत अध्ययन में आलोच्य काल में निम्नलिखित ग्रन्थ प्रकाश में आये।

14. श्री विनयचन्द्रसूरि विरचिता कालिकासूरि कथानकम् रचना संवत् 14वीं शताब्दी।
15. श्री महेश्वरसूरि (पल्लीवाल गच्छीय) विरचिता कालिकाचार्य कथा, लेखन सं. 1365.
16. श्री प्रभाचन्द्रसूरि विरचितं प्रभावक चरितान्तर्गतं कालकाचरितम्।
17. पं. श्री हरिरत्न रचित कथानक।
18. श्री जिनदेवसूरि विरचिता कालिका सूरि कथा, रचना संवत् 14वीं शताब्दी।
19. श्री माणिक्यसूरि विरचिता कालिकाचार्य कथा।
20. श्री देवकल्लोल उपाध्याय (श्री मद्केशगच्छीय 1566 संवत्सरे) कालिकाचार्य कथा।
21. श्री समयसुंदर उपाध्याय (1666 सं. श्री बृहतखरतरगच्छे) कालिकाचार्य कथा।
22. श्री शुभशीलगणि विरचिता भरतेश्वर - बाहुबली वृत्यन्तर्गता कालिकाचार्य कथा सं. 1509
23. श्री धर्मदासगणि विरचिता उपदेश माला टीकान्तर्गता कालिकाचार्य कथा।
24. श्री सिद्धर्षि रचित कथा।
25. श्री सोमसुंदर सूरि विरचिता उपदेशमालान्तर्गता कालिकाचार्य कथा, सं. 1457-93.
26. श्री रामचन्द्रसूरि विरचित कालिकाचार्य कथा।
27. श्री गुणरत्नसूरि (पिप्पलगच्छै) विरचिता कालिकासूरि कथा, रचना 16वीं शताब्दी।
28. मलधारि हेमचन्द्राचार्य विरचिता पुष्पमालान्तर्गतं कालिकाचार्य कथानकम्।

- गृहित- श्री कालक कथा संग्रह

"ज्योतिर्विदाभरण" नरमक ग्रन्थ के अनुसार इस विक्रमादित्य के दरबार में जो नौ रत्न सुशोभित करते थे, उनमें एक था क्षपणक"।

धारणा है कि यह क्षपणक और नहीं होकर जैन आचार्य सिद्धसेन दिवाकर भी एक चमत्कारी जैन आचार्य थे।[1] जैन अनुश्रुतियों के अनुसार उन्होंने महाकाल मंदिर में विक्रमादित्य को ज्योर्तिलिंग के फटने पर पार्श्वनाथ के दर्शन करवाये थे।[3]

चाहे यह घटना अविश्वसनीय लगे इतना तय है कि ईसा की निकट शताब्दियों में मालवा जैन धर्म का एक प्रमुख केन्द्र रहा था।

शक कुषाण युग में अनेक युग प्रधान आचार्य भी हो चुके हैं जिनमें भद्र-गुप्ताचार्य, आर्य-वज्र तथा आर्य-रक्षितसूरि के नाम गिनाये जा सकते हैं। आगम साहित्य को आर्य-रक्षितसूरि ने चार भागों में विभक्त करके जैन धर्म की दृष्टि से इस युग के ऐतिहासिक महत्त्व को और भी बढ़ा दिया है।

संदर्भ

1. धन्वंतरिक्षपणकामरसिंह शंकु वेतालभट्ट घटखर्पर कालिदासाः।
   ख्यातो वराहमिहिरो नृपतेः सभायां रत्नानि वै वररूचिर्नव विक्रमस्य।।
   - ज्योतिर्विदाभरण, 22.10.
2. प्रभावक चरित, प्रबंध चिन्तामणि, प्रंबध कोश, विविध तीर्थकल्प, विक्रमचरित आदि ग्रंथों के अनुसार।
3. क्राउझे : पूर्वोक्त, पृ. 402.

विक्रमादित्य विषयक जैन साहित्य की सूची

क्र. सं.	रचना समय	ग्रन्थ नाम	रचियता
1	2	3	4
		1. संस्कृत मौलिक ग्रन्थ	
1.	सन् 1233	पंचदंडात्मक विक्रमचरित्र	अज्ञात
2.	13वीं-15वीं शती	सिंहासनद्वात्रिंशिका	क्षेमकर
3.	सन् 1414 लगभग	विक्रम चरित्र	कससहृदगच्छीय उ. देवमूर्ति
4.	सन् 1433	विक्रम चरित्र (पंचदंड)	साधु पूर्णिमा रामचन्द्र सूरि
5.	सन् 1433	विक्रम चरित्र (सिंहासन द्वात्रिंशिका)	साधु पूर्णिमा रामचन्द्र सूरि
6.	सन् 1442	विक्रम चरित्र	तपागच्छीय शुभशील
7.	सन् 1467	सिंहासन द्वत्रिंशिका	धर्मघोषगच्छीय राजवल्लभ
8.	विक्रमचरित्र	राजमेरू	
9.	विक्रमचरित्र	इन्द्रसूरि	
10.	विक्रम पंचदंड प्रबंध	पूर्णचन्द्र	
		2. प्रबंध संग्रहों के अन्तर्गत सामग्री	
11.	सन् 1277	प्रभावक चरित्र	प्रभाचन्द्रसूरि
12.	सन् 1304	प्रबंधचिन्तामणि	मेरूतुंगसूरि
13.	सन् 1348	प्रबंधकोष (चतुर्विंशति प्रबंध)	राजशेखरसूरि
14.	13वीं से 15वीं शताब्दी	पुरातन प्रबंध संग्रह	अज्ञात

3. लोकभाषा में विक्रम विषयक जैन साहित्य

1	2	3	4
15.	सन् 1442	विक्रम कुमार रास	वडतपागच्छीय साध कीर्ति
16.	सन् 1508	विक्रम सैन चौपई	पूर्णिमागच्छीय उदयभानु
17.	सन् 1539	विक्रमरास	तपागच्छीय धर्मसिंह
18.	सन् 1581	विक्रमरास	आगम विडालंबगच्छीय मंगल माणिक्य
19.	सन् 1665	विक्रमादित्य चरित्र	तपागच्छीय मानविजय
20.	सन् 1657	विक्रमसैन चौपाई	तपागच्छीय मानसागर
21.	सन् 1667	विक्रमादित्यरास	तपागच्छीय परमसागर
22.	सन् 1680	विक्रमादित्यरास	खरतर दयातिलक

4. विभिन्न कथाओं को लेकर रचित स्वतंत्र लोकभाषा की कृतियां

(क) वैताल पच्चीसी

1	2	3	4
23.	सन् 1536		सोरठगच्छीय ज्ञानचंद
24.	सन् 1562		तपागच्छीय देवशील
25.	सन् 1589		खरतर हेमाणंद
26.	सन् 1593		बड़च्छीय मुनिमाल
27.	सन् 1615		तपागच्छीय सिंहप्रमोद

(ख) पंचदड चौपाई

1	2	3	4
28.	सन् 1499		अज्ञात
29.	सन् 1503		सिंहकुशल
30.	सन् 1526		विनयसमुद्र
31.	सन् 1593		वडगच्छीय मुनि मालदेव

1	2	3	4
32.	सन् 1671		खरतर लक्ष्मीवल्लभ
33.	सन् 1676		खरतर लाभवर्धन
34.	सन् 1773		तपाभाण विजय
(ग) सिंहासन बत्तीसी चौपाई			
35.	सन् 1462		पूर्णिमागच्छीय मलयचन्द
36.	सन् 1541		ज्ञानचंद
37.	सन् 1554		उपकेशगच्छीय विनयसमुद्र
38.	सन् 1559		बिवंदनीकगच्छीय सिद्धसूरि
39.	सन् 1582		खरतर हीरकलश
40.	सन् 1621		तपासंघ विजय
41.	सन् 1691		खरतर विनयलाभ
42.	सन् 1614		अज्ञात
(घ) विक्रम-खापरा चोर चौपाई			
43.	सन् 1506		खरतर राजशील
44.	सन् 1666		खरतर अभयसोम
45.	सन् 1670		खरतर लाभवर्धन
(ङ) विक्रम-चौबोली चौपाई			
46.	सन् 1667		खरतर अभयसोम
47.	सन् 1705		खरतर कीर्तिसुंदर
48.	सन् 1713		पल्लीवालगच्छीय हीरानंद
(च) विक्रम-लीलावती चौपाई			
49.	सन् 1559		कक्करसूरि शिष्य
50.	सन् 1671		खरतर कुशलधीर

1	2	3	4
(छ) विक्रम-कनकावती चौपाई			
51.	सन् 1707		तपा कांतिविमल
(ज) विक्रम-शनिश्वर-रास			
52.	सन् 1631		तपासंघ विजय
53.	सन् 1679		धर्मसी

स्रोत : श्री जैन सत्यप्रकाश : विक्र विशेषांक, पृ. 183-187

(C) Pure Literature Works

There are several literary works written with the motive of displaying literary skill but they also throw some light on history. The great authors Bhāsa. Vātsyana[20], Kālidāsa, Śūdraka, Varāhamihira and Bāṇa, seem to be associated with Ujjain in one way or another. Bhāsa, in some of his plays, speaks of Ujjaiyinī and gives graphic description of its palaces, mansions, temples, gardens, lakes, pleasures and comforts.

From the *Mālavikāgnimitra* of Kālidāsa, it is known that Puṣyamitra deputed his son Agnimitra as his governor at Vidīśā. His son Agnimitra had to fight Yajñasena, the ruler of Vidarbha. This work also refers to the conflict between Vasumitra, son of Agnimitra, and the Yajñasena in connection with horse sacrifice. Śūdraka's *Mṛcchakaṭika,* one of the most interesting dramas in Sanskrit literature, gives a vital and realistic picture of Ujjain. The same is the case with the *Padmaprābhṛitakam* and the *Pādataditakam* which were probably written at Ujjain. Varāhamihira, who belonged to *Kapithā* now identified with Kāyatha near Ujjain, is the author of *Bṛhatsaṁhitā* which is a veritable mine of useful information on different subjects.

Some of the stories of the *Prabhāvaka Carita* informed that Śālivāhanas and Vikramāditya were contemporary and Śālivāhaana defeated Vikramāditya I in the last years of his reign. The Jaina Harivaṁśa Purāṇa by Jinasena give sufficient information of the early rulers of Avanti. The *Jaina paṭṭāvalis* give us correct chronology of the rulers of Ujjain which is useful for the history of Vikramāditya and Śakas[21].

Legends grew around the great personality of Vikramāditya and a large number of literary works were written. The Kālakācārya-Kathānaka inform us not only about Vikramāditya, but also about the early advent of the Śaka into Western Malwa from Seistan via Sind and Kathiawad, in the second century B.C. Besides, the *Kathā-sarit-sāgara* written by Somdeva. *Siṁhaśanadvātriṁśilka Vetālapañcaviṁśati* and *Sukasaptati,* describe the qualities of Vikramāditya. The Jainas have preserved the traditions of Vikramāditya in many literary works such as Prabhāvakacharita, jaina Harivaṁśa Purāṇa and *Paṭṭāvalis,* and the Vamstalies are somehow useful for the history of Vikramāditya.

(D) Saṁvatas (Eras)

Saṁvatas have played an important role in reconstruction of the cultural history of Vikramāditya. These were used for counting years. This *Saṁvata* has been founded by Vikramāditya in 57 B.C. and this is very important era. This *Saṁvata* has been divided into four branches chronologically. The names are Kṛta, *Mālavā, Vikrama* and Sogiṇa. Among them Kṛtia is the earliest and indicates figuratively Golden age (*Saty Yuga*). The monuments discovered have been engraved in inscriptions with years. These years seems to be Kuṣāṇs *Saṁvata*.[21]. Kaniṣka was the founder of this *Saṁvata. Śakas* are known to have recognised the suzeranity of the Kuṣāṇs. Similarly, the Śaka *Saṁvata* originated in 78 A.D. and its founder was Chasṭana. The rulers of this *Saṁvata* also played an important role in the history of Ujjain.

III. Writings of Foreigners

In addition to archaeology and literature, writings of foreigners sometimes give interesting information regarding the ancient history of Malwa. The unknown author of the *Periplus of the Erythraean Sea*, made a voyage to the Indian coast in about 80 A.D. and left a record of its ports, harbours and merchandise. Ptolemy wrote a geographical account of India in the second century A.D. The *Geography of Ptolemy* mentions Ujjaiyinī as the capital of West Malwa of *Trastenes*, undoubtedly a Greek corruption of the name Chasṭana.

REFERENCES

1. *ACTR*, pp. 94, 111, 121 and 130.
2, *MTA*, p. 29.
3. *The Monuments of Sāñchī*, p. 283.
4. *Sel. Ins.*, p.78.

5. *EI,* II, no. 190.
6. *Ibid.,* pp. 158-159.
7. *KHT,* p. 60-61.
8. *IAR,* 1953-54, p. 63.
9. *ASI,* 1913-14, p. 227.
10. *ASC,* VI, p.178.
11. *MTA,* pp. 156-165.
12. *lbid.,* pp. 158.
13. *Jaina Dharma kā Itihas,* volume II, p. 415.
14. *Vikrama Viseshanka,* pp. 183-187.
15. *Iibdi.,* pp. 400-413.
16. *The Monuments of Sāñchi.*
17. *Sel. Ins,* p. 78.
18. *EI,* XXVII, pp. 252ff.
19. *Ibid.,* XXIII, pp. 42-52.
20. P.C. Bagchi holds the view that as Vātsyāyana appears to have been thoroughly acquainted with South-Western India, he most probably lived in Ujjain in the fourth century A.D. This town was a great centre of literary activity, and was connected with distant countries both overland and across the sea. This contributed largely to the opulence of the city, and its cosmopolitanism. This type of city must have attracted *nāgarakas* of the type described by Vātsyāyana (See *Kāmasūtra,* the Hindu Art of Love, Trans and Edit by B.N. Basu).
21. *MTA,* K.C. Jain, pp. 32-33,

Chapter 3

Ancestry and Early Career of Vikramāditya

Introduction

Vikramāditya was born in *Mālavā* republic which seems to be the earliest and popular. They came from outside as Parthias and Scythians. There are stages in the settlement of the *Mālavās.* In the first stage during the fourth century B.C., they settled along with *Kṣūdrakas* in the Indo-Greek land. From there, they migrated to Punjab and settled there. From Punjab, they migrated towards Rajasthan and Malwa. In Malwa, they established their kingdom. The *Mālavās* elected their leader known as Gardabhilla or Mahendrāditya who was his father. Thus, he belongs to *Gardabhilla* family and this family was also the branch of *Mālavā.* Then, they were also of foreign origin.

(i) Birth and Early Career: The birth of Vikramāditya took place in Ujjain. He became gradually popular by his name Vikramāditya, and his title Vikrama.

(ii) Education: The education given to Vikramāditya was similar to the princes of his times. Vikramāditya got his education at *Sandipaṇi* in Ujjain which was the great seat of learning. It seems that the early career of Vikramāditya to the greater extent was the same as other important rulers who flourshed in this age, such as Khāraveḷa, Rudradāmana and Chasṭana. Besides his education at *Sandipaṇi,* Vikramāditya got all necessary education from the Jaina Saint Kālakācārya. As a result of it, Vikramāditya became king of versatile personality.

According to the Digambara Jaina *Paṭṭāvalīs,* Vikramāditya played as a child for eight years, for sixteen years, he roamed over the country. From the *Kathā Sarita Sāgara,* we get much information about his education. His father Mahendrāditya made the best possible arrangement for the education of his son. His education started after his tonsure, and his first lesson was given in alphabets and numerals. His serious schooling started at the time of his initation ceremony (*upanayana).* Vikramāditya received education in the art of both peace and war.

From the *Kathā Sarita Sāgara,* it seems that this early career as a prince became a pattern followed by the nation. From history, it is known that, Khāraveḷa, Rudradāmana and other princes followed it as a pattern.

Khāraveḷa of the Chedi family of Kaliṅga was brought up by his father in systematic way. He followed the foot-steps of Vikramāditya.

When Khāraveḷa was a prince, he played different games defeating the prince of young age with the lovely body and fair brown complexion. He bore the noble and auspicious bodily marks. As a prince, the Hāthigumphā inscription represents him as one who was *Lekha* (writing), *Rūpa* (Coin), *Gaṇanā* (Accounts), procedure and law expert and had proficiency in all the branches of learning.

Rudradāmana belongs to the Śaka family and his ancestors came out from Sindh, and others outside the country. His father and grand father were able kings and gave Rudradāmana education in different branches of learning.

Rudradāmana was not only conqueror and administrator but a patron of classical Sanskrit. He was himself a master of grammar, politics, music and logic. He was reputed for the excellence in the composition of prose and verse in Sanskrit. Under him, the city of Ujjain became one of the most important seats of learning in India. Similar type of education subsequently followed by the king, proves *Vikramāditya* as a historical figure.

(iii) Marriage and Wives: According to the *Kathā Sarita Sāgara,* when Vikramāditya reached the marriageable age, a number of proposals came for his marriage. These types of proposals had political importance and were customary in India, so it was proper for his father Gardhabhilla Mahendrāditya to arrange the marriage of his son with the daughters of the defeated rulers.

According to the Junagarh inscription Rudradāmana attended several *svayaṁvaras* and won the hands of a number of princess. These matrimonial alliances of Kāmdamakas find the gradual absorption of the Scythians to the Indian society.

Gautamīputra Sātakarṇī seems to have made an attempt to save a few conquered territories by contracting a matrimonial alliance with the Kārdamakas. As known from the Kanheri inscription, that Vāśiṭhiputra, the son of Gautmīputra, was husband of a daughter of a Mahākṣatrapa Rudradāmana after this event; Rudradāmana further claims to have defeated Sātakarṇī, lord of Dakṣiṇāpatha for the second time which he did not destroy as he was a near relative.

(iv) A Great Calamity: The Mahendrāditya (Gardabhilla) family wanted to establish in India, but a great calamity fell upon the Śakas. It appears the Mahendrāditya (Gardabhilla) had some success against the Mechchhas on the frontier of Sindh before the major calamity. It seems the Mahendrāditya was over-powered by the Mechchhas. The Jaina sources are already very clear on this point. The *paṭṭāvalies*, the *Niṣithasūtra* and *Prabhāvaka Carita* all record the defeat and expulsion of Gardabhilla (Mahendrāditya) by the *Śakas.*

(v) First Śaka Invasion of India: The calamity was the first Śaka invasion of India in the first century B.C. This fact is independently esatablished, by the ancient histories of some countries. It was the time when the Śakas had moved to Scythian and they had also occupied the trans-indus part of Sindh. These circumstances of the Śakas coincided with the religious dispute between the Śakas and the Jainas. Gardhabhilla (Mahendrāditya) had to face difficulties when he was in exile. But soon after the exile, Mahendrāditya became powerful and acceded the throne. Vikramāditya succeeded in establishing his rule in Avanti. After the retirement of Mahendrāditya, Vikramāditya obtained power. In course of time, his subject duly anointed him here to his realm, and himself retired. Vikramāditya had to face many problems. His main problem was the raising of an efficient army and to organize a war against the Śakas intruders. All the Jaina prabandhas describe the financial difficulties of Vikramāditya and his firm determination to collect the necessary money.

The main aim of Vikramāditya was the restoration of power in Avanti, and the firm foundation of the Mālavā republic. Vikramāditya was a young man of iron determination, and doubtless courage. The Jaina *nibandhas* contain a number of stories to prove his courage. He concentrated all his energy at the defeat of Śakas and devoted himself to the preparation of war against them.

(vi) Exile and Tribulations of Gardabhilla Mahendrāditya: According to Jaina sources. Gardabhilla Mahendrāditya was in exile and in the course of it many difficulties arose according to Brahminical sources. Mahendrāditya was alive when Vikramāditya succeeded in establishing the rule in Avanti. He was of great valour, and believed in the subjects who duly anointed him heir of his realm.

(vii) Plight and Preparation of Vikramāditya: As a result of the Śakas occupation over Avanti, Gardabhilla or Mahendrāditya put his entire family at a safer place for protection. Vikramāditya was a promising boy, and a great future awaited him. Vikramāditya started preparation for war.

He was raising an efficient army, and organize a war against the Śakas intruders. This scheme required sound finance and Vikramāditya was put to a great strain in this matter. All the Jaina *prabandhas* described the financial difficulties of Vikramāditya and his firm determination to collect money. These efforts of Vikramāditya can be compared with the similar effort of Cāṇakya in collecting money in order to raise an army to fight against the Nandas.

(viii) The Allies of the Mālavaā: The first Śakas invasion of India was not only a calamity to the Mālavās but a great obstacle to the existence of other states in neighbouring areas. The *Mālavās* formed only a link in the great chain of republican people, who occupied over the areas of Eastern Punjab, Rajputana, Ākāra, Avanti, Sindh and Saurāṣṭtra. Archaeological and literary evidences prove the existence of a number of republican states in this area in the first century B.C. This also proves Vikramāditya who allied with these states was himself a historical figure, and was also the founder of Vikrama era. We can briefly introduce these republics as follows :

(a) The Yaudheyas (South-east part of Punjab).
(b) Mādras (North-eastern Punjab).

(c) The Śibis (Nagari near Chittore).

(d) The Ārjunāyanas (Rajasthan) on the coins of these republics are found an inscription Arjunāyana Jaya (Victory of Arjunāyana).

(e) The *Utsavasaṁketas* (Ajmer in Rajasthan).

(f) The Śūdras were easily defeated by the Śakas, but they survived as people.

(g) The Ābhiras were originally in Sindh, and they were of Śaka pressure.

(h) The Kukuras belong to Saurāṣṭra, they were subjected by the Śakas.

(i) The Vṛiṣṇis : In the first century B.C. in Saurāṣṭra, their coins are found in this part of country. These coins bear the inscription of the first century B.C. "*Vrṣṇirājanaya Gaṇasya trōtasya*" (of the Vrṣṇirājanaya-Gaṇa, the protector of the country.

(j) The Rājanyas : They occupied the territory near Mathurā.

(k) The Mahārāja Janapada.

(l) The Vamarathas.

(m) The Sālaṅkayanas.

(n) The Audumbaras : The coins are found in north Punjab.

(o) The Mālavās : The Mālavās and Kṣūdrakas in the early period occupied south western part of Punjab and they formed a confederation against the Greece.

The Mālavās had a number of sub-coins, one of them was in possession of Avanti, and others were in south-eastern Rajasthan and eastern Malwa. After the first Śakas occupation of Avanti in 71 B.C. and the second occupation in 78 A.D. the bulk of the Mālavā remained in south-eastern part of Rajasthan. The majority of the republics originally belonged to the Punjab. The republics of Rajasthan became powerful not only in Rajasthan but their power and prestige increased in Malwa, Saurashtra and Sindh. The republics were always hostile to foreign invaders, and gave heroic resistance. These republics fought against the Śaka invaders of India from about 300 B.C.

The Śaka mention was more serious than the first one in many aspects. The part played by these republics was more striking and glorious than their ancestors in Punjab. The first Śakas invasion of India was a stormy event, and took place all of a sudden.

(ix) The Restoration of Avanti and the Firm Foundation of the Mālavā Republic: Vikramāditya firmly tried to regain Avanti, and establised his people more firmly there. Vikramāditya had to face many difficulties and trials in order to strengthen his position. Vikramāditya concentrated all his energy on the defeat of the Śakas and devoted himself to the preparation of war. He was encouraged and helped by his constant companions.

Vikramāditya had to rely on his own people, the *Mālavā* for war. He seems to have formed confederacy against the external danger.

(x) The Expulsion of the Śakas: The Mālavās formed a confederacy against the external danger of Śakas. Vikramāditya organized an effective confederacy of the *Mālavās*, *Kṣūdrakas* and others. This confederacy consisted of the terriotory of Rajasthan, Central India and Eastern Punjab. It was a great achievement on the part of Vikramāditya to march towards Avanti where he defeated the Śakas who wrongfully occupied Ujjaiyinī. The war between the republican forces and the Śakas must have been serious. According to athe *Kāḷakācārya Kathā,* told in *Prabhāvaka Charita,* some time after the Śakas occupation of Ujjaiyainī, Vikramāditya uprooted the family of the Śakas. A similar narration is found in the *Vicāraśreṇi* of Merutuṅgācārya after the lapse of some time. There will be a chief named Vikramāditya, these statements are corroborated in the *Paṭṭāvalīs.* According to them, the reign of Gardhabhilla Mahendrāditya was followed by the Śakas rule for four years in Ujjaiyinī. Then he was succeeded by his son Vikramāditya.

(xi) Foundation of National Era: The defeat of the Śakas was a historic event of the checkered career of the country. The country was freed from foreign dominions and the oppressive rule of the Śakas.

This event was a result of the combined effort of a number of republican people in which the Mālavās took the leading part. The success of Vikramāditya over the Śakas entitled him to his *Viruda* (epithet) *Śakōri* (means enemies of the Śakas). It was one of the important epithet of *Vikramāditya.*[1] The event inaugurated an age of peace and prosperity which was figuratively called *Kṛta* (Sata Yuga - Golden Age). In order to commemorate this land mark in, Indian history an era was founded. In the beginning, this era was known as *Kṛta,* because it investigated figuratively the *Kṛta* age (Golden age) at the time of the firm foundation of the *Mālavā* republic after the expulsion of Śakas and later on, it was called the era of *Mālavā* republic or the era of the *Mālavā* people of the *Mālavā* era of the *Mālavā* lords. Ultimately, by the end of the ninth century A.D., the era began to be called the era of Vikrama or the era of King Vikrama. How this transformation of this name of the era took place has already been explained. There is no doubt that the chief responsbility in the foundation of the era was that of Vikramāditya. The Jaina and all popular traditions are unanimous on this point. Kālakācārya in his work mentions of establishing this era.

The current astronomical traditions include the name of Vikrama in the list of great founders of Indian eras.

But being the head of a republic under the constitutional law of the state, he could not lend his name to the era. Though in popular mind, his name was always remembered in connection with the era. The name of Vikramāditya survived the loss of republician traditions in India.

(xii) Issuing of Victory Coins: Another important device for perpetuating the great success of the republics over the Śakas was the minting of victory type of coins. These were memorial coins. A large number of coins have been discovered which bear the legend "*Mālavā Gaṇasya Jayaḥ*" (Victory of the Mālavā people or Victory of the Mālavā republic). The compatriots of the Mālavās, the other republic of Rajasthan, central India and the Punjab also followed the Mālvās and instituted the victory type of coins.

REFERENCE

1. *V.U.*, p. 102.

Chapter 4

Vikramāditya and His Era

Introduction

Vikramāditya was the President of the Mālavā Republic. He defeated the Śakas, and in commemoration of his victory against the Śakas, he started the *Vikrama Saṁvata*. Thus, both Vikramāditya and his *Saṁvata* are historical. Based on his personal life, the *Paṭṭāvalīs* also throw light on his historicity. The Dholpur inscription of ninth century A.D. mentions the *Vikrama Saṁvata* for the first time. The Aulikara inscription of Naravarmana dated 419 A.D.added the title Vikrama to the name of the king. This shows that the name and fame of the early Vikrama still continued. *Kṛta, Mālavā, Aulikara* and *Maukharī* were added together after some time. At Raidh, inscribed coins, seals, and inscriptions with legends of *Senāpati* are found in place of the king. The seals with the republican inscriptions of his age have been discovered at Raidh.

Coins have been found at Ujjain with Ujjaiyinī symbol.

City type coins of Ujjaiyinī, Mahiṣamati, and Vidiśā coins have been also found. "*Mālavānām Gaṇasya Jaya*" coins belonged from the second century B.C. have been found at Mālavā Nagara. It continued upto 1000 A.D.

Explored and excavated cities such as Ujjain, Kayath and Navada Toli give an idea of the coins of second century B.C.

Cities Associated with the Vikrama Saṁvata: Some scholar think that this *Saṁvata* was current in Pōrthia and Punjab, but it is wrong. It is found in Rajasthan and Malwa even today.

There are different names of Vikrama and Vikramāditya. Some of them are individual names, some have titles, some belong to dynasty and some are ideal names. All these proved that Vikramāditya was the historical name and he founded the Vikrama era in 57 B.C.

Mālavā Gaṇa is the oldest *Gana* of the country, and it indicates territory and population. Vikramāditya was the name of the President of this republic, and the head of the republic began to be called Vikramāditya. Vikramāditya is known to have defeated the Śakas and in honour of his victory, he was awarded with the *Vikrama Saṁvata.*

The *Mālavā* seem to be the oldest republic of India and the name of its chief was Vikramāditya. There are other saṁvata of different names but identical in number. The names and number of these saṁvata are as follows :

1. *Kṛta* era 282 Nāndsa
2. *Kṛta* era 284 Barnala
3. *Kṛta* era 295 Badwa
4. *Kṛta* era 428 Vijaygadh (Bayānā)
5. *Kṛta* era 461 Mandsor
6. *Kṛta* era 480 Gangadhar
7. *Kṛta* era 481 Nagori

Aulikara Saṁvata

1. 417 A.D.
2. 532 A.D.

Mālavā Saṁvata also continued along with *Śaka Saṁvata.* This also prove the historicity of both Mālavā and Vikramāditya.

Mālava era

1. 461 era
2. 589 era
3. 795 era
4. 936 era

Vikrama era

1. 898 era
2. 973 era
3. 1005 era
4. 1008 era
5. 1028 era
6. 1099 era

From Uniyara, it is known that Mālavā Gaṇa is found mentioned on the legends of coins of the second century B.C.

The earliest inscription seems to be called *Kṛta* and is found at Nāndasā in Rajasthan. The term *Kṛta* indicates the golden age.

The term Mālavā indicates Janapada (territory and population) as found on Mālavā inscription near Mandsor. The above inscription indicates that the Vikrama *Saṁvata* and its branches originated from the *Saṁvata* 57 B.C., but disappeared by 282 A.D. In this way there is a vaccum of three hundred years. Inscriptions of Vikrama era and its branches are noticed. At this time, Śakas became very powerful and the *Mālavās* became weak and they gradually disappeared. The *Vikrama Saṁvata* again revived from the ninth century A.D. as known from the Dholpur inscription.

From the Vikrama *Saṁvata* and Śaka *Saṁvata*, it is known that Vikrama *Saṁvata* was popular in north India while Śaka *Saṁvata* was well known in South India, and in astronomical works.

The Vikrama *Saṁvata* originated in 57 B.C. The Mālavā Janapada was in existence, but no direct and continuous evidence about its origin is available. It is also known that *Kṛta*, Mālavā and Aulikara had identical origin of their *Saṁvata*. The *Kṛta Saṁvata* originated in Rajasthan and most of the inscriptions of the Vikrama *Saṁvata* are found in Rajasthan and some are found in Malwa. The name of the *Saṁvata Kṛta* seems to have originated from some auspicious incident. *Mālavā Saṁvata* originated from the *Mālavā Janapada* and Aulikara *Saṁvata* from some connection with the light.

Thus, it is clear that after defeating the Śakas. Vikramāditya started the *Vikrama Saṁvata* in 57 B.C. and made himself the President of the *Mālavā* republic.

The Gupta rulers Samudragupta and Chandragupta II originated their title from the *Vikram Saṁvata* of Malwa. D.R. Bhandarkar and D.C. Sircar are of this view, but it is not correct. Rulers of different dynasties have used this *Vikrama* title.[1]

Writings of Foreigners: The Greek writers supply valuable information about the ancient republics in Northern India, and it is also known from the *Kālakācārya Kathānaka.* Jainism was prevalent in Western India on the eve of the coming of the Śakas. The Jaina monks and nuns were found in western India in such a number that they caught the attention of the foreigners.

Vikramāditya is known to have diplomatic relations with the foreigners such as the Yavanas and Kuṣāṇas in North, Śakas and Hūṇas in South.

REFERENCE

1. *V.U.*, p. 260.

Chapter 5

Historicity of Vikramāditya

Introduction

There is a great controversy among the scholars about the historicity of Vikramāditya. These scholars have advocated some arguments against the historicity of Vikramāditya.

1. The name of Vikramāditya is not associated with the Vikrama era from the time of the foundation and during the early centuries.
2. During the early period of Vikrama era, the astronomers do not use and mention in their works, rather they date their composition in Śaka era.
3. There is no contemporary literary and archaeological evidence to prove the existence of Vikramāditya historically.
4. The ancient inscriptions found in Malwa, Rajputana and neighbouring areas disclose that the earliest name of the era was *Kṛta*.

5. There are legends, traditions and popular stories regarding the Vikramāditya but no substantial historical evidence has been advanced.
6. The existence of Vikramāditya is just like Rāma, Kṛṣṇa, Bimbisāra, Ajāta Śatru and Nāndasā etc. It is difficult to prove his existence like above rulers.
7. For the continuous three hundred years, we do not find the name of Vikramāditya, but *Śaka Saṁvata* occupied its place and became powerful.
8. For proving the historicity of any king, his time and place are important factors. Unless these are available, we can not prove his historicity.
9. Two strong objections have been raised by Rajbali Pandey. It has been argued that the name of Vikramāditya has not been found with the era 57 B.C.

It became necessary because the Śakas started their own *Saṁvata,* and began to name it. No substantial contemporary evidence has so far been discovered along with Vikramāditya. The reason for this is unassuming character wherever it has been mentioned. It was the practice in ancient India not to give their name for propogation. Śakas considered Vikramāditya to be the greatest enemy. They wanted to finish the era and the name of Vikramāditya. Therefore, they have taken this extreme step.

Arguments in Favour of Historicity: There are arguments in favour of the historicity of Vikramāditya.

1. It is true that there are no solid contemporary

arguments for historicity but we find near contemporary historical material for the historicity of Vikramāditya. For historicity, we have to rely on such facts.

2. When we call Ajātaśatru, Bimbisāra, Chandragupta Maurya as historical figure, there should be no difficulty in accepting the historicity of Vikramāditya.
3. From the archaeological point of view, the period from the first century B.C. to the second century A.D. was the golden period, in which ideal persons contributed to all round development. Chaṣṭana, Khāraveḷa, Kaniṣka or his successors, were great contemporary rulers of Vikramāditya. If we compare Vikramāditya with them, there is no difficulty in accepting his historicity. The date of reigning period and the date of the era mentioned in connection with the ruler chronology prove his historicity.

Vikramāditya had versatile personality and many sided virtues proves that Vikramāditya existed, and contributed in different spheres.

Archaeology (inscriptions, coins and literature) also prove the historicity.

The early Brahaminical works (*Bṛhat Kathā Mañjarī)* belongs to the first-second century A.D. They indirectly prove the historicity of Vikramāditya.

His inscriptions of *Kṛta Saṁvata, Mālavā Saṁvata* and *Aulikara* also prove that Vikramāditya was a historical figure and followed republican traditions. It means that historical facts were followed by Vikramāditya.

The coins of different types (*Kārṣpaṇa)* Punch-marked, City coins, Māḷavā coins and inscriptions with *Senāpati* also prove that the history of Vikramāditya was based on coins.

The administration of Vikramāditya was based on *Arthaśāstra* of Cāṇakya. Vikramāditya enforced his principles. This proves the historicity of Vikramāditya.

The society, economy, art and architecture, education, science and literature of his period were promoted by Vikramāditya, and it was due to his historical sense.

The Jaina Nirvāṇa Kāṇḍ, a Paṭṭāvalī proves the historicity of Bimbisāra and Ajātaśatru. There are placed much earlier than Vikramāditya. If this is so, we should also consider Vikramāditya to be a historical figure.

For the historicity of Vikramāditya, corroborative evidence has been advanced. It proved to be very useful. Just as the date of Kālidāsa has been fixed by this method, we should also attempt such methods of literature and archaeology to prove the historicity of Vikramāditya.

The name of Vikramāditya is found in the works of Astronomy, but not in the other books of later times. Actually, it does not affect the historicity of Vikramāditya. *Vikrama Saṁvata,* Gupta *Saṁvata,* Śaka *Saṁvata,* Śalivāhana *Saṁvata* and even their branches were associated with Vikramāditya.

All the above factors prove that Vikramāditya started Vikrama era in commemoration with some great achievements. It was the greatness of Vikramāditya that he did not give his name clearly in literary works, inscriptions, coins and archaeological findings. If critically examined, some other facts will come to light.

To ignore such an ideal ruler, with several achievements, it was not proper. Actually, Vikramāditya is great figure in history.

The two Śaka foreign invasions have been referred in Brahiminical and Jaina literature and outside India.

A large number of coins have been discovered with legend *"Mālavā Nāma jayaḥ"* and these facts prove historicity of Vikramāditya. Here the name of the ruler is not given.

In the seal of Vikramāditya, the name of the *Senāpati* has been engraved in place of the king. This proves the historicity of Vikramāditya.

The struggle in the south among the Śakas, Sātavāhanas, Khāraveḷa and Vikramāditya proves the historical figure. In this struggle, Śakas emerged successfully and ruled over for three hundred years.

Rajbali Pandey has discussed different theories about the historicity and also his own views. Rajabali Pandey came to the conclusion that *Vikramāditya* was historical figure and lived in the first century B.C.

K.C. Jain also discussed the Vikramāditya problem as a myth after discussing different theories. Now, he changed his views and considered it to be a historical personality living in the first century B.C. It seems that *Mālavā* kingdom of Vikramāditya and Ujjayinī as Śaka-capital surpassed even those of other rulers of India and outside, both in time and place. His reign was based on democratic principles. He emphasized his rule on the basis of moral principles, Therefore, his republican kingdom could survive for such a long time.

The continuation of two *Saṁvata* side by side such as Vikrama and Śaka also proved the historicity of Vikramāditya.

The use of the title *Vikrama* by Gupta rulers and rulers of the south also prove the historicity of Vikramāditya.[1]

Wrong methods have been adopted for surpassing his power by his enemies but they could not gain success (4th century to 7th century A.D.) but his name itself disappeared for some time. But actually it was not so. His measures of ideal administration immortalizes him for ever.

In conclusion, the historicity of Vikramāditya may be proved as follows:

1. Like other rulers, the historicity ofVikramāditya can be proved in space and time.
2. There is lot of archaeological material such as coins, inscriptions and terracottas of the time of Vikramāditya. There is a numismatic evidence with the legends "*Mālavā Nāma Gaṇasya Jayaḥ*" on his coins. These coins are attributed to Vikramāditya.
3. The era of 57 B.C. stands for Vikrama Saṁvata, and it stands for Vikramāditya.
4. The different branches of *Vikrama Saṁvata* such as *Kṛta, Mālavā* and *Aulikaras* stand for Vikramāditya.
5. The Jaina literature and Paṭṭāvalis also prove the historicity of Vikramāditya though it is of late

period.

6. The republican traditions of Vikramāditya are still followed.
7. The name Malavā Nagara of Raidh in the tenth century A.D. proves the existence, the continuity of *Mālavā* republic and also proves the historicity of Vikramāditya. The name and title Vikrama is found in some coins of Samudragupta and Chandragupta II and, this title in the inscription of the Aulikara ruler Narvarman, may also prove the historicity of Vikramāditya. There is a long list of kings in India who adopted the title of *Vikramāditya,* Kumar gupta, Skandagupta, Vikrama VI, Cālukya and Vikrama Cōḷa. The tradition of adopting the title of Vikramāditya continued up to Hemachandra Vikramāditya. Hemu one of the Muslim writers who opposed the Mughal forces in the second battle of Panipat in 1555 met a tragic, but heroic death.[2]

There is a great controversy among the scholars about the historicity of Vikramāditya. No doubt there is a lot of literary and archaeological evidences to prove the existence of Vikramāditya. Gradually, the knowledge advanced and people thinking became scientific. They have become successful in proving the historicity of Vikramāditya. They have also advanced evidence but still people are not convinced. There views against historicity are as follows :

The current theories mentioned are :

1. Fergusson's theory.
2. Kielhorn's theory.
3. The theory of Cunnigham and Fleet.
4. Marshall's theory
5. V. Gopal Aiyar's theory (Gautmīputra Sātkarṇī).
6. Jayaswal's theory(Vikramāditya).

We have examined evidences derived from various sources — Indian era, popular stories, the literary traditions of the Hindus and the Jainas, epigraphy, numismatics, the history of Mālavās and the history of the Śakas. When taken separately they may not be conclusive and their authority may be questioned. But when, they are set together, they converged towards the central fact the existence of the Vikramāditya in the first century B.C. and thus established the truth of Indian tradition about him. Available evidences lead us to the following conclusion :

1. Vikramāditya is not fiction but a historical figure who flourished in the first Century B.C.
2. He belongs to the Gardabhilla branch of the Mālavā people, who migrated from the Punjab to Avanti.
3. He was the president of *Mālavā* republic (*Mālavā-Gaṇa-Mukhiyā).*
4. The capital of *Mālavā* republic in thefirst century B.C, was Ujjayinī and Vikramāditya ruled here.
5. He drove the first Śakas invaders out of India in 57 B.C.
6. The great event of the Śaka defeat was celebrated by the foundation of era, which during its early

century was called *Kṛta* and *Mālavā Saṁvata* and later on came to be known as Vikram Samvata.

7. To commemorate the success of the Mālavās against the Śakas, victory type of coins were also issued.
8. Vikramāditya was an ideal and popular ruler. He was reknown patron of the literature and art.[3]

The modern scholars like K.C. Jain and others have examined the different current theories of modern scholars and came to the concluison that Vikramāditya is not a myth but a historical figure. It is essential to note that there are two groups of historians. In one view, it has been realised that Vikramāditya was a historical figure who lived in Gupta period during the fourth century A.D. The other view is that Vikramāditya lived in the first century B.C. and founded *Vikrama Saṁvata.* All these different views have been thoroughly examined by Dr. K.C. Jain in his book "*Malwa Through the Ages.*" It is further to note that one and the same authors like K.C. Jain gave different views at the same place at different times.[4]

K.C. Jain, Raj Bali Pandey, K.D. Bajpai, D.R. Bhandarkar, D.C. Sircar, K.P. Jaiyaswal and A.S. Altekar have advanced modern view of historicity.

REFERENCES

1. Pandey, Rajabali, *Vikramāditya of Ujjaiyini*, p. 260.
2. *Ibid.*
3. Pandey Rajabali, *Vikramāditya of Ujjaiyinī*, pp. 49-50.
4. *M.T.A.*, 156.

Chapter 6

Comparative Study of Vikramāditya

Introduction

From the history, we know about the occasions which led to the war, dreadful things such as famines diseases, and scarcities. Such activities can be reformed by following the methods of Vikramāditya.

H.G. Wells[1] has written the history of the world in which he tried to prove Aśoka as one of the greatest rulers of the world. This is clear from his teachings of Buddhism propagated by him. Aśoka says there is no higher duty than the welfare of the whole world. Aśoka's ideal was not simply the brotherhood of men but rather the brotherhood of living beings. It is the whole animate world with which he himself feels connected and his supreme duty lays in securing them not only from temporal but also spiritual welfare. He esatablished hospitals both for men and animals. He appoined officers for the propogation of his religion. He followed the policy of religious toleration. All men were equal before him. On these principles, he was regarded as a great ruler.

As regard to Aśoka's confession of the ideal that guided him and shaped his line of action, this is correct representation and not an over statement and may be seen from the sort of the assures, he adpated to realize his object. First, in regard to the physical happiness which was common to both the men and the women and second in best welfare activities. But we know he strained every nerve to promote spiritual well being also that is to say to generate and disseminate *Dhamma* among the whole of mankind not simply among the people of his own empire but also outside India. Vincent Simith and D.R. Bhandarkar followed the views of H.G. Wells.

Prof. Rhys Davids[2] holds Aśoka was like Constantine because just the religious benefications of the later were the cause of the spiritual decay of the Christian Church.

Aśoka's conversion to Buddhism and his munificent endowment to the *Saṁgha* was the first step on the downward path of Buddhism as well as of our country.

Prof. Rhys Davids tried for the propagation of Christianity, just as Aśoka tried for Buddhism.

Aśoka with Marcus Aurelius Antominus: A third ruler whose name coupled with that of Aśoka is Marcus Aurelius Antominus. In respect of private noble life, there can be no doubt that he was Aśoka's equal and in point of mental culture was even superior. But in regard to the sublimity of the ideal, the display of their unflagged and well directed zeal, the Buddhist monarch surpasses the

Roman emperor. He inflicted systematic persecution on Christianity in the country. He exerted himself strenuously and systematically for the good not only in the whole creature-world, and racial, national or family pride or more in his life of self assessment. Aśoka has been compared by one writer to a good by many other princes such as King Alfored Charlemagne, Omar Khalif-I. There were many kings who were warriors or great emperor, or great administrator, like Aśoka but what entitles Aśoka world-wide and ever lasting fame is the temporal and spiritual good of the people that he accomplished. The only other rulers therefore, whose name is worth mentioning along with him, is Akbar.

Aśoka and Akbar: There can no doubt Akbar strove very hard for the welfare and happiness of his subjects but the particular point in which he resembles, Aśoka is the religious toleration he granted. But it is to be remembered that Akbar, a man of word, and was in no mood to endanger his sovereignity for the cause of religious truth. When Akbar proclaimed the divine faith, there was also the welfare of self-glorification behind it.

Estimation of Akbar and European Historians: In the estimation of European historians, Alexander the Great, Ceasor and Napolean are the world's greatest monorch. But Mr. Wells most pertinently ask "What were there permanent contributions to the humanity. He drank hard and murdered ruthlessly." Ceasar and Napolean may have done immense good to his country, but as far as their obligation to the human race is concerned they are practically 'nil'. As regard Aśoka we know what vision he was gifted and how profound it was. The brotherhood was not simply of human but of living being. He was over powered with the vision of promoting the physical happiness and moral elevation of the whole world.

Aśoka and Saint Paul: In the history of Buddhism, Aśoka's importance is second only to that of the founder of that religion. Saint Paul can be compared to Aśoka. It is true the message preached by Jesus was for all people but its universal character was appreciated and emphasized by his eminent followers. It was Paul who broke the barriers of race and law which were harming it. Paul declared "there is no door where there is no wall, every partition has been broken down, every restriction and division among men in the sight of God has been abolished". The law of the God is as all embracing as the sky above us. His grace is as free as the air we breath. In Jesus Christ, there is neither Jew nor Greek bound, nor free male nor female. Similarly in Aśoka's time Buddhism had almost degenerated into a local provinical sect. He destroyed the barriers which detached one sect from another, by teaching principles and tenets and thus promoted the essence of religion which they all share in common. There can be no doubt in this matter, the royal teacher arose to a higher level then what Buddhist Piṭakas attained. Aśoka was not a patron but hermitable apostle of Buddhism.

Kaniṣka was also the great ruler because he ruled

inside and outside India. Some scholar recognize Kaniṣka as a founder of the year after his name. He greatly propogated Buddhism.

It has been discussed above the important kings of the world. But no one has so far made any mention of Vikramāditya of Ujjaiyinī. Vikramāditya also did not mention about himself. No body has given the cause of omission of the history of Vikramāditya for three hundred years. Here partisan attitude has been noticed, Vikramāditya has been discussed from all points of view. Impartially up till now several works regarding him have not been studied. There is no mention of Vikramāditya in the history of the world. After such a long time it is necessary to study again the history of the world along with Vikramāditya from all points of view.

Vikramāditya ruled for sixty years but during the last years of his reign, his decline started. It was due to the fact that he suffered reverses in the south from the Sātavāhanas as known from the Jaina *Paṭṭāvalīs*.

The first golden age of our country from the first century B.C. to second century A.D. and revival of the golden age from 8th century to 12th century A.D. is also due to Vikramāditya. Unfortunately, it remained hidden and gained not so much name and fame as it should have been.

After three hundred years this name of Vikramāditya was again revived. Thus, we can prove the greatness of Vikramāditya.

Vikramāditya was inspired by Candragupta Maurya, as an administrator for the first time. Besides we have discussed above great kings of India and outside India. They became famous because of their achievements. Some of them extended their empire by conquests with the establishment of efficient administration, some partonised art, literature, sciences, education and justice. Vikramāditya surpassed all great rulers of the world by his versatile genius and many sided virtues.

The foundation of Vikrama-era in 57 B.C. and the name of Vikrama indicates that he was wounderful personality. His conquests and personality brought prosperity to the nation. Unfortunately, all these have been suppressed. Proper historical investigation is necessary to investigate his achievements. He was an ideal ruler of the world. Revival of his greatness after three hundred years is confirmed by history. For the first time, he established republican traditions in our country and these traditions still continued in unassuming form.

Vikramāditya is famous for his *Saṁvatu* not only in India but also in the World. It started in 57 B.C. which we may call it the golden period. It shows importance of the time of Vikramāditya as he was a great person. It also indicated contemporary rulers of his time, Khāraveḷa, Kaniṣka, Gautamīputra and Sātakarṇī etc. It is also called Kṛta age, which mean golden age. There was all-round prosperity in this age. There were enemies of Vikramāditya also, as a result his progress was retorted.

We have discussed the history of the rulers, their decline was due to the fact that they did not follow the policy of religious toleration and adopted Buddhism and Christianity. This weakened them. Besides their administration was not efficient. On the other side, Vikramāditya prove to be the ideal ruler from all points of view.[3]

Up till now, the history of the world has not been rightly connected with Vikramāditya. Vikramāditya was highly influenced by Kālakācārya and he became an ideal ruler. He emphasized an ethical principles of religion. Vikramāditya was also influenced by the right faith, right knowledge and right conduct. His policy influenced his subjects as well as, *Saṁgha* and five *Aṇuvratas*. Vikramāditya rightly patronised art, literature and sciences. He inspired the people to follow *Pañca Mahā Vratas, Ahiṁsā, Satya, Ācārya, Brahmacharya* and *Apṛgraha*. The success of Vikramāditya, as a ruler, was due to policy patronised by him.

REFERENCES

1. H.G. Wells, *The History of the World.*
2. Prof. Rhys David, *Buddhist India*, London, 1902.
3. *V.U.*, p. 102.

Chapter 7

Conquests and Extent of Empire of Vikramāditya

Introduction

Vikramāditya was a great conqueror. The *Kathā Sarita Sāgara* describes the victorious camp of Vikramāditya joined by the king of Śaktikumara of Govda, Jayadhvaja of Karnataka. Lāta Sunandana of Kashmir, Gopāla of Sind, Vindhyaballa of Bhills etc. This is mainly regarded as fictituous because these names of rulers and places are not confirmed by any independent contemporary evidence. It is possible that he might have extended his empire by conquering some neighbouring places.

(i) Pursued by Śaka Invasions: The wars compelled the republican Mālavās under Vikramāditya to give up battles. The expulsion of the Śakas from Avanti was not enough, but also from Rajasthan. The Śakas were lingering in

Aparānta (Northern Konkan) *Saurāṣṭtra (*Kathiawar and Sindhu) in the neighbour-hood of India on the Western frontier.

(ii) Literary Description of War and Conquests: In the Brihant *Kathā Mañjarī* there are sporadic references to the military exploits of Vikramāditya. Vikramāditya easily conquered all. The *Kathā Sarita Sāgara* gives a more detailed and connected account of the wars and conquests of Vikramāditya.

A number of small republics became free. These are eastern Punjab, Rajputana, Malwa, Saurāṣṭra and Sindh and they were regaining their power and prestige. The Bactarian Greeks in the extreme North-West became weak by these republics. Pārthians and Śakas got pressure from the West.

(iii) Compaign from Outside India: There is reference to the compagin from outside India. The foreigners have been mentioned. The *Bṛhat Kathā Mañjarī* and *Kathā Sarita Sāgara* were present in the vicinity of India in the first half of the first century B.C. Their existence was challenged by Vikramāditya and he faced them with courage. The foreign invasions took place in India by the people like Yavanas (Greek) from North, the Kuṣāṇa, Śakas and Hūṇas which created chaos in the country. The second Śakas invasions was also held soon.

(iv) Comments on the Victories Camp of Vikramāditya: The *Kathā Sarita Sāgara* seems to give comments of the victorious camp of Vikramāditya, but some scholars do not agree because these names are not found in the dynastic history of the respective provinces. The description should be regarded as fictituous and useless.

The great conquest described in literature of Vikramāditya is confirmed by archaeological evidence.

(v) Kālidāsa, court poet of Vikramāditya has tried to compare these conquest with Raghu of Kālidāsa. It should be remembered that the poet was not recording the contemporary political and military events of his times but composing an epic based on the events which had taken place long before him.

(vi) Parallels of Vikramāditya Digvijaya: It is also held that Vikramāditya has tried to compare Raghu but is not proper.

(vii) The Nature of Vikramāditya's War: It is held that the wars of Vikramāditya did not aim for annexation of countries and extension of the empire. His aim was not to build an empire but to establish political supremacy over numerous small states of India. He wanted political co-ordination of the country, without involving any harm to the subdued states. This policy was the compromise between the imperial character of military operation and the republican traditions and local freedom of the people. This explains whyVikramāditya is regarded as an ideal ruler. He is still respected and remembered by the people of India.

A terrible battle took place between Vikramāditya and Śālivāhana, and Vikramāditya destroyed the army of Śālivāhana.

We should try to co-relate the conquest of *Vikramāditya* as described in some literary works with the other sources. By doing so, we get information about the conquest of Vikramāditya.

Khāraveḷa was the great contemporary king of Vikramāditya. He was also a conqueror. The Khāraveḷa inscription gives information about his conquests. It seems that he started the compaign from the south with his large army. Some times he conquered the king Sātakarṇī, and some times he released showing diplomatic relations. He also in course of expedition seems to have occupied the capital of Vidyādhara. He also seems to have subdued the Rāṣṭriyakas and Bhojakas in the Berar region. Khāraveḷa destroyed Govardhanagiri, a hill fortess of Barābara hills and attacked the city of Rājagṛiha. The news of this expoilt of Khāraveḷa caused so much terror in the heart of Yavana king that he fled away to Mathurā. The Yavana ruler whose name is mentioned some times was probably later Indo-Greek ruler of the eastern Punjab. Khāraveḷa also destroyed the city of Pithvaḍa the capital of Machalipaṭṭam in the Mādraṣ state. He threaten the rulers of Uttarapatha (North-West India). He also defeated the king of the Magadha people possibly on the Bank of Gaṇgā. The name of the king given is Brahaspatimitra in Prākṛt. Kings of Magadha in order to revenge the humiliation of the Kaliṅga during the time of Nanda and Mauryas, carried out booty from Aṅga and Magadha. Together with certain Jaina images originally taken from Kaliṅga, he also defeated the Pāṇḍya king of the south. This inscription of Khāraveḷa for the first time gives reliable description of conquests.

Kaniṣka

It was only Kaniṣka who ruled both inside and outside India. His capital in India was Peshawar. Out side province were Yārkanda, Kashagar and Khotan with capital at Gandhāra. The country became rich from different points of view. He introduced *Kṣatrapa* system to rule over Malwa. Malwa seems to be a subordinate province of the Kuṣāṇas. His period of reign, was epoch making. In India, there was a development of literature. As far as art, literature and religion are concerned, Mathurā became the greatest centre of Jainism in his time.

Rudradāmana

The source of information of Rudradāmana is the Junagarh inscription. It is the most important monument of ancient India. From this inscription, we know that the Chaṣṭana was grandfather of Rudradāmana. This is corroborated by the evidence of coins. It seems that Chaṣṭana was *Mahākṣatrapa* and Rudradāmaṇa was *Kṣatrapa.* He recovered most of the northern districts of his dominians originally conquered from Nahapāna. In the Junagarh inscription, this ruler is represented as a lord of many countries. Including Aṅkara, Avanti, Anūpā, Aparánāta, Saurāṣṭra and Ānarta which had all been conquered from Sātakarṇī in 130 A.D. probably when Rudradāmana was a *Kṣatrapa* under his grandfather. Rudradāmana who claims to have defeated twice. Sātakarṇī became the lord of *dakaṣiṇā* patha. He did not destroy him because he was a near relative. Vāśiṣṭhiputra was the son-in-law of Rudradāmana. Rudradāmana claims to have reinstated deposed kings on certain reference *feudatory* of Nahapāṇa. These are out-stated by Rudradāmana. The *Mahākaṣtrapa* territory comprised such as Kutcha, Malwa, Kathiawada, Gujarat, Northern Kokan and Mahiṣamatī conquered from Sātakarṇī, lord of *Dakṣinā patha,* at the time of accession. Later, it included the districts such as Kutcha, Sabarmati, Valley, Maru, Sindhu-Soviera, Niṣāda. Rudradāmana appears to have ruled over the whole of Kṣarata dominion with only exception of Nasik and Poona districts. He conquered all these territories by his own valour.

Rudradāmana is said to have inflicted crushing defeat on the republic Yaudhāya. It is identified with Bayana.

Gautamīputra Sātakarṇī

He is said to have been the destroyer of *Kṣatrapa* dynasty to which ṣaka chief Nahapāṇa belonged. Nahapāna over there must have taken place in or shortly of the eighteenth regnal year of Sātavāhana king and after 125 A.D. which is the last known date of Nahapāṇa. In the Nasik inscription of eighteenth of the Gautamīputra reign record the grant of some land whcih was previously in possession of Vāṣavadatta son-in-law of Nahapāṇa and was governor of Southern provinces. It is interesting that the order regarding grant was issued from the victory camp of the army that was gaining the success and that Sātavāhana king represented as stationed at the time of place called Baitaka, the Govardhana district. Apparently Gautamīputra Sātakārṇī in that region as the head of the army was connected with his campaign against the *Kṣatrapa* which led to the liberation of not only the upper Deccan but also of considerable part of western and central India. The grant of the village called Korika in the Namal Anara (Jaina district) made by Vāśavadatta and after-words by Gautamīputra Sātakarṇi, to the transference of the territory which was under Gautamīputra. According to Nasik *Praṣasti, Aparānta, Anūpa, Saurāṣṭra, Ākara* and *Avanti* must have been conquered by Nahapāṇa. Further, Gautamīputra in the Nasik district shows how the Sātavāhana king captured the *Kṣatrapa* territory and restrict the later coins for recirculation.

Just as Vikramāditya is regarded as an imaginary figure by some scholars. Similarly, the conquest of the Vikramāditya are not regarded in reality. This seems to be not correct. Actually, Vikramāditya did not conquest the vast territory with army and wealth but he conquered the heart of the people and became immortal in history. We should consider his conquest and extent of the empire in the sense of *ahiṁsā* but not in the sense of violence, in which great harm is done to people in the sense of men and land etc.

Chaṣṭana

Chaṣṭana was the founder of the Kadamaka dynasty of the Śakas. Chaṣṭana seems to be the most powerful ruler of the Śaka dynasty.

He also extended his empire by his conquests and Ujjain became prosperous during his reign. He maintained relations with the out-side country.

Conclusion

The different sources give an idea about the conquests and extent of the empire of Vikramāditya. Literary sources are fictitiuous, and they cannot be reliable unless they are confirmed by independent evidence of epigraphy and coins. After critical examination it may be concluded that the conquests of the Vikramāditya may extend further. Vikramāditya was contemporary of Khāravela and Rudradāmana.

When Mauryan empire became weak the out line provinces rose in revolt and became independent. Their authority was not acknowledged even by their ministers and generals. The great Puṣyamitra Śuṅga, who probably belong to Avanti, usurped the throne from Bṛhadratha, the last Maurya emperor in 187 B.C. For time being he arrested the disintegration of the Mauryan empire. Soon after his death, the feudatories and provincial governors became independent, taking advantage of the situation. The Śuṅgas shifted their capital from Pāṭalīputra to Vidiśā. Later on, the Sātavāhanas of the south extended their power in Malwa by destroying the Śuṅgas and Kāṇvas.The Kuṣāṇanas are known to have extended their way over some territory in Malwa through their Kṣatrapas. The western Kṣatrapas of Ujjain gradually became independent. A long struggle continued from time to time between Sātavāhanas and the Western Kṣatrapas. In the end, the Sātavāhanas were defeated. The Nāgas, the Bodhis and the Māghas established their independent kingdoms. The western Kṣatrapas ruled for a long period of three hundred years.

Chapter 8

Tribal States

(THE ŚUṄGAS 187-75 B.C., PUṢYAMITRA 187-151 B.C.)

Introduction

The tribal states of India may be divided under three heads : A. Monarchial states, B. Republican states and C. Wild Tribes. Now, we first take the Monarchial states.

A. Monarchial States

1. Bṛhadratha: He was the last Mauryan emperor who was murdered in the presence of the army by the Brāhmaṇa, Commander-in-chief Puṣyamitra, became the founder of the Śuṅga dynasty. The first event of his reign was his conflict with Vidarbhas. He had also to face the Greeks invasion of Indo-Bactrian rulers Demetrious and Menander. He performed two horse sacrifices. According to the *Divyavadana,* he was a prosecutor of Buddhism. Puṣyamitra was succeded by his son Agnimitra who had the experience of governing Vidīśā as Viceroy under his father. Agnimitra's son Vasumitra in his earlier days defeated theYavanas. The Indo-Greek king Antilkidas of Taxila sent his ambassador Heliodorus, son of Dion (Diya) to the court of the Śuṅga ruler the Bhāgavata or *Kāsipūtra Bhāgabhedra.* The Kaṇvas also as Brāhmaṇas seized power in about seventy-two B.C.

2. Kuṣāṇas : Kaniṣka was one of the greatest ruler of the Vikramāditya period as known from the Kuṣāṇa inscriptions and monuments found in Mathurā. The Kuṣāṇa had their kingdom at Mathurā. It was ruled over by Kuṣāṇas. Rulers Kaniṣka, Huviṣka and Vāsudeva were important. Among the Śaka rulers of Mathurā, Rajivlal and Hegema are note-worthy. As known from the Mathurā antiquities, Jainism was the most imortant religion. It was followed by the carpenters, ironsmiths, merchants etc. The numerous Jaina antiquities of this period were found in Mathurā.

3. Śakas : After the downfall of the Mauryas, India fell a victim to foreign invasions. The early advent of the Śakas into Western Malwa, from Seistan via Sind and Kathiawad, in the second century B.C. is known from the *Kālakācārya Kathānaka.* After establishing their hegemony in Saurāṣṭra and Kathiawad, they penetrated into Malwa. On the basis of traditions, Rajbali Pandey suggested that there was a ruler named Vikramāditya in Avanti during the first century B.C. He defeated the Śakas who invaded India for the first time in the first century B.C. In order to commemorate this event, he inaugurated a new era in 57 B.C. called *Vikrama Saṁvata.* He was a great conqueror as well as a patron of art and literature. On the other hand, D.C. Sircar does not regard Vikramāditya as a historical figure because there is no contemporary evidence for his existence.

4. Khāraveḷa : The most important monarchial kingdom was the Kingdom of Kaliṅga, ruled by the Chedi ruler Khāraveḷa in second or first century B.C. Khāraveḷa was one of the remarkable figures of the time of Vikramāditya. He seems to be contemporary of Vikramāditya. He has friendly relation with his contemporary rulers. As a ruler, Khāraveḷa thought of the welfare of his subjects and he spent large amount of money on this account. He employed efficient machinaries for good administration. He convened a conference of learned Jainas and consolidated the Aṅga which was the sacred text of Jainism. Like Aśoka, he was tolerent in matters of religion.

It seems that two families Kṣaharāta and Kārdamakas of the Western Kṣatrapas ruled over Western India as Kṣatrapas of Kaniṣka-I and his successors. Afterwords, they became independent. *Nahāpana* of the Kṣaharāta family became independent, and also conquered some territories, in about 124- 125 A.D. He seems to have been defeated by the Sātavāhana ruler Gautamīputa. Sātakarṇī. Chaṣṭana, the founder of the Kārdamaka family, established his capital at Ujjain. Chaṣṭana and his grandson Rudradāmana defeated the Sātavāhana ruler Gautamīputra Sātakarṇī and conquered several territories. Some times after 130-131 A.D., Rudradāmana, succeeded to Chaṣṭana as Mahākṣatrapa. From the Junagarh inscription dated 150 A.D., he seems to have become a powerful ruler and claims to have extended his empire by his conquests. These Western Kṣatrapas rulers ruled for about three hundred years, till their power was finally crushed by Chandragupta II. According to the Jaina traditions, *Nahapāna* after being defeated from Gautamīputa Sātakarnī he retired and became the saint by the name Bhūtabali (66-90 A.D.). He performed very important work of editing the Jaina *Āgamas* and completed it in 75 A.D. by the name of *Ṣaṭakhaṇḍā grantha.* In the inscriptions of the second century A.D. there is mention of the names of those persons who got *Kevala Jñāna.* This inscription is the earliest in this connection.[1]

5. The Sātavāhanas: According to the Paurāṇic traditions, as well as the coins of the Andhra Sātavāhana dynasty which began with Śimukha who destroyed the remains of the Śuṅga power and liked the Yavana king Suśarman in 27 B.C. Śimukha Sātavāhana is also known from the coins. Several Sātavahana rulers are known from the *Paurāṇas* but it is only athe last nine rulers of the Puranic list whose historicity is supported from coins. It appears from the coins that the Sātavāhanas came in to prominence as independent rulers only after the fall of Śuṅgas Kāṇvas. Their capital was Pratiṣṭhāna (Paithana). It is known from the Nasik inscription that Gautamīputra Sātakārṇī, one of the later Sātavāhana kings, defeated

Nahapāna of the *Kṣahārata* dynasty and annexed his territory to his kingdom in 124 A.D. Vāiṣthīputra Śrī Pulumāvī, successor of Gautamīputra Sātakarni married the daughter of Western Kṣatrapa Rudradāmana of the Kārdamaka family. Another notable Sātavāhana ruler after Vāiṣthīputra Pulumāvī Guptamīputra Yājña Śrī Sātakarṇī (173-202 A.D.) who seems to have conquered back some of the lost territories from the Western Kṣatrapas. The Sātavāhana dynasty came to an end in about 225 A.D.

6. Nāga Kingdom : Nāgas ruled over their kingdom Vidiśā, Kantipuri (Kautiwar) and Padamāvati (Pawāya). *Vṛṣhanāga* is known to be the Nāga ruler of Vidiśā, some times in second century A.D. Their arose the dynasty of Nāgas which lost in all probability by the fourth century A.D. Their capital was Padmāvatī where the large number of coins have been found.

7. Guptas and Aulikara: The early Guptas rulers extended their power upto Vidiśā. They fought against the Śakas, Aulikaras and the rulers of other tribal and republician kingdoms in the neighbourhood.

These Aulikaras seems to have been a branch of Mālavās because they always used the *Mālavās* era in their inscriptions. Even in the Bihar-Kotra inscription, this era has been called the "*Aulikara Samvata.*" These Aulikaras seems to have been responsible in giving the name of this territory as *Mālavā.*

CHAṢṬANA AND HIS ŚAKA SAṀVATA

According to Furgussan, Thomas, Benarji, Rapson and Jaiswal Kaniṣka started the Śaka era beginning in 78 A.D.[2]

Smith and several other scholars thought that Kaniṣka rule began in about 125 A.D. and ended in the second half of the second century A.D.

Chaṣṭana could not start the Śaka era because Periplus does not mention it. *Śaka Saṁvata* might have been started by Nahapāna. According to Jaina literature he ruled for forty years, but we find the inscription of Nahapāna of the year forty six *i.e.* he could not be the founder of Śaka era. Wimakadphises could not start this era because no coins and inscriptions possess this date refered to this era. The only king who established this era was Kaniṣka.

We have Chālukyan inscription mentioned in Vikrama *Saṁvata* which mention that this era was started by Śaka ruler in 78 A.D.

The continuous recalling of the king of Kaniṣka-group namely, Kaniṣka-first, second and third, Vaṣiṣaka 24-28, Huvikuṣaka 24-60, Vāsudeva 67-78 shows that Kaniṣka was a founder of Śaka in 78 A.D. as attributed by many scholars.

If we place Kaniṣka towards the beginning of the middle of the second century A.D., it is possible Kaniṣka was not the founder of this Śakas era because he has not mentioned in his coins and inscriptions. It seems that he has mentioned the year of his reign.

There is controversy about the date of Śakas *Saṁvata* and the authority which issued it. Other rulers such as the Kujula Kadphises, Wimakadphises, after Kaniṣka and Huviṣka, it is also held by some scholars that Śakas ruled as feudatories of the Kuṣāṇa. These coins show the year of his reign, Śaka era started in 78 A.D., but this view is not correct. No Śaka name is found on these coins. Inscriptions found on sculptures etc. do not mention the name of Śaka era.

Śaka era is found on the Śaka coins, the Sātavāhana's coins and other rulers of the south mention the year of their reign. The coins with the Śaka names, other inscriptions etc. definitely prove that these were issued by the Śakas. They mentioned the name, title and date of the Śaka rulers. These coins were issued continuously for three hundred years by Śaka rulers. This proves that Śaka rulers became powerful and defeated the Mālavās. Sātavāhana coins were also issued in Śālivāhana era. Śaka era was started by other ruling dynasties of the South. The difficulty is that who started the Śaka era. R.C. Majumdar is of the view that this Śaka era was issued by Chaṣṭana. He was the most powerful ruler of this dynasty. Ptolomy's geography of Egypt, mention Chaṣṭan as the king of Ujjain.

It seems Chaṣṭana was the founder of Śaka era. Two inscriptions of the Śaka year, eleven and fifty two were discovered at Andhav in Kachchha. The inscription of eleven Śaka era should be regarded as the earliest epigraph of the family. Another Andhav inscription shows that in the Śaka year one hundred thirty and one hundred thirtyone, Rājā Chaṣṭana was ruling.

The Junagarh inscription dated seventy two Śaka era supplies information about the conquests. An important role played by the dominion of Chaṣṭana in Sino-Roman and Indo-Roman commerce. Chaṣṭana became so famous emperor that had been sculpted as evidenced by a sculpture now in the Mathurā Museum. It was perhaps meant for worship in Devakulekha.[3]

Jaina tradition also confirmed that Śaka emperor started Śaka era in 78 A.D.

The grandson of Chaṣṭana named Rudradāmana was no less in achievement than Chaṣṭana. He extended his empire by conquests. He was a great ruler and promoted welfare activities for the people, and he was also himself a great scholar. He maintained diplomatic relations with his contemporaries.

B. Republican States

In the kingdom of Vikramāditya, there were republican states. Among them, *Mālavā* was the earliest and most powerful and with Ujjain as its capital, Most of the republics settled in Punjab, but gradually migrated to Rajasthan and Malwa. They gradually became powerful, some-times *Kṣūdrakas* and Mālavās formed confedration (Saṁgha). The important republics were as follows — Mālavās, Śibis, Arjunāyana, Uttama-Bhadras, Mādras, Yaudheyas etc. In these republics, we find virtues, but in some we find limitations. Among these republics, the *Mālavā* republic was very important. When the Greeks attacked India, they formed confederation with

Kṣūdrakas. They migrated to Mālwa, and became very powerful. They spread in wide area, and established separate kingdoms. They fought against the internal enemies. They formed their own constitutions. They issued their own coins. Similarly, the Arjunāyanas had their own coins. The capital of the Śibis was *Mādhymika* near Chittore. From the first century B.C. to the third century A.D., they increased their power and maintained law and order in their kingdoms. There were certain virutes in these republics.

The ancient Indian republics were highly praised for their working.

These republics were powerful. They held full and frequent assemblies. This showed the spirit of co-operation among the republics. They acted in accordance with ancient customs. These republics carried out the advice of the elders, gaining their experience. No women belonging to them were detained by force or abducted. They honoured and revered the *Chaitayas.* The followers of different religions were free to practice. This spirit of Catholicism made these republics really strong. The ancient republics used to give great emphasis on moral values. A high sense of justice was maintained by them. Without it, no republics could last long. Discipline was another virtue of the republics. Bravery was a point of ambition, and honour among the people. Equality prevailed among the Gauṇas. All persons were equal before the law. They also laid emphasis on equality. A great reason of their political strength was that the republic was nation in arms. They were a citizen army, and therefore they were superior to the hired army of monarchy government. The Greek writers also described such republics with considerable military vital principles of their constitution. These ancient republics were also born to form *Saṁgha* or league.

These republics had administrative virtues. They were successful in their financial administration. Their treasury remained always full. They issued coins, but without name following their early traditions.

In spite of their virtues, these republics gradually disappeared. The imperial rulers brought their down fall by the policy of territorial expanison. The invasion of foreigners was no less factor in crushing the free spirit of these republics. We know from the Nasik inscription of Nahapāna that he sent Vāsavadatta to fight against the Mālavās who rose in remote area. From the inscription of Rudradāmana, we know that he crushed the power of the Yaudhayas. The smallest was weakness of some of the republican states. The destructions and dissensions were the internal dangers to these ancient republics.

The President of the Yaudheya republic has been mentioned in the Bayana inscription dated 300 A.D. Republics are of two types : In one, they assumed even the title of president or king. In the second category, they assumed the title of Gaṇa but not the title of king.

There were also territorial republic head who assumed the title of feudatory or king.

The king of this period were of peculiar type because of peculiar circumstances. The rulers of territorial title division and officials assume the ordinary title and circumstances.

Some times they assumed clearly the title of the king Badwaha inscription of king, Mokhari inscription of king. During the age of Vikramāditya, the conception of Navaratna, knowledge of perfection and *Nirvāṇa* arose. Under these circustances how can we think of other personality during his age. Thus Vikramāditya was the great personality of his age.

C. Wild Tribes

There were also wild tribes in existence as known from inscription. Rudradāmana conquered wild tribes from the Sātavāhanas which were again restored by the Sātavāhanas. These tribes were Ahhiras, Maeras (Bhelsa and Jhāñsī area). There were also wild tribes such as Kakas, Kharaparika (Damoh district), Prorjunasa and Sanakanikas. They were near the forest areas of Vindhyas. Therefore, these are known to be wild tribes.

While dealing with the history of the Yaudheyas, the *Purāṇas* state that taking their own off shoots, there will be six contemporary dynasties of the Andhras which will be listed as follows :

1. The Andhra-bhṛtyas.
2. The ten Abhiras.
3. The seven (ten) Gardabhilas (Gardabhilas).
4. The ten Śakas.
5. The eight Yavanas.
6. The fourteen Tukharas, thirteen Maurvndas and eighteen Maunas.

Most of these wild tribes seem to have continued their old traditions similar in some aspects to the republics.

REFERENCES

1. K.C. Jain, *Jain Dharma Kā Itihāsa,* p. 413.
2. *V.U.*, pp. 51-76.
3. *Kalidas and His Times,* K.C. Jain, p. 61.

Chapter 9

Administration

Introduction

The administration of Vikramāditya was efficient. He introduced changes in the administration prevalent since the time of Chandragupta Maurya. It has been compared to *Rāmarājya*. This type of administration is also known as *Lok Rañjan* or *Prajā Rakṣā*. He also introduced the decentralization of administration by giving powers to provinces, districts and villages.

The characteristic of our ancient Indian political ideas was that of their wonderful continuity. Its foundation was laid in our ancient values.[1]

The administration of Vikramāditya was based on the *Arthaśāstra* of Kauṭilya but he introduced innovations. The general features of the administration remained the same. Vikramāditya, Khāraveḷa and Rudradāmana introduce certain changes.

Ujjain became the capital of Vikramāditya, Vidiśā continued as the capital of the ruling dynasties and its importance continued in different ways.

General Features of the Administration

The general features of the administration remained the same. The empire was divided into territories governed by superintendents looking after them. There was Council of Ministers to look after the administration. There was decentralization of administration and it is noticed in the administration of trade, commerce, mines, foreign-affairs and agriculture. The empire was divided into provinces, districts and villages. There was judicial system. There were courts for civil and criminal cases. Vikramāditya remained famous for his judicial and financial system. From Megasthanese, we know about municipal administration in Pāṭalīputra. It seems that Vikramāditya and others also introduce the same system. There was also *Pañchāyata* system in villages. There was custom and excise system for the increase of the finance of the centre. There was a department for external affairs also.

It is remarkable to note that Vikramāditya carried the administration of the state through *Adhyakṣas* who carried on the administration of the kingdom and undertook the industries and trade on behalf of the state. The superintendent of the agriculture had to supervise agriculture, irrigation and manure. He encouraged settlelment and formation of new villages. They also controlled trade and commerce of the state.

Decentralization of Administration

There was remarkable decentralization of administration because the empire was divided into provinces such as Saurashtra and Malwa. These were governed by the governor and they were responsible for protecting their territories against external invasion and internal disorder. Provinces were divided into *bhukits* (districts) officers in charge known as *Uparikās* who were appointed by and responsible to the emperor himself. The district administration enjoyed considerable power. The popular element had a large voice in the district administration. The Chief Banker, the Chief Artisan, the Chief Viṣaya figured in the Council-officers in charge of district who were reponsible for maintaining law and order and collecting government taxes and revenue. They were assisted, in this task, by a large staff with different qualification. In addition to the official court of the province and district a large number of popular courts were there. Guilds of traders and caravans had their own courts. Pañcāyat-courts in towns and villages tried civil and petty criminal cases.

Village and Town Administration

Village was the pivotal of the administration. *Grāma-Adhyakṣā* was the head of the village assisted by the village council. There was town-administration carried on by the officers of the town, They imposed many taxes like land tax, revenue tax and octroi duty. There were taxes on manufactured articles. The state claimed ownership in waste land, forest, pastures and salt-mines.

The central government worked efficiently and kept well informed about the happening in the districts and villages. Lands were carefully measured. There was safety of the subjects both from the foreign and internal disturbances. Government was not content merely with promoting material prosperity of its citizens but also moral and spiritual welfare. Peace and prosperity secured by the government, led to a rich and remarkable development of art, literature, philosophy and sciences.

Foreign Policy

There were foreign states existing round about the kingdom of *Vikramāditya*.There were Khāraveḷa, Śakas, Greeks, Parthians, Kuṣāṇas etc. The king maintained diplomatic relations by treaties with these states. The *Yavanas* sent their ambassador to Vidisha. There were treaties with Śakas. The king Khāraveḷa sent his ambassador to the court of Demritrius of Mathurā. He also maintained diplomatic relations with the Kuṣāṇas ruling in his times. In dealing with these states, he adopted the foreign policy based on maṇḍala-siddhānta in order to deal with these foreign states with territories. The main policy was to maintain some sort of balance of power and to assert his own.

The foreign policy was determined by the geographic and economic environment of the other states. The extensive regions favoured the growth of large state but there was difficulty of transport and communication. The big state could not stay for long. The relation with different foreign states can be maintained by the *Maṇḍala* theory with treaties.

The aim of *Maṇḍala* theory was to determine the aims of foreign policy and relation with other states. Enforcement of treaties was also necessary. There were more or less regular diplomatic relations of Vikramāditya with other states. The above policy of Cāṇakya become popular by name. But it was enforced in actual practice during the time of Vikramāditya. The content of the Vikramaditya administration is as follows :

Welfare Activities

Vikramāditya was the king of great generosity. He promoted welfare of his subjects in many ways. He constructed roads in his kingdom and planted trees on road side. He also built hospitals in his kingdom where medicines was given to the people. He also gave food and drink to the people.

Justice

Vikramāditya was famous as fountain of justice. He is accessible to any body at any place and at any time for hearing without any objection. Below king there were court known as *Dharmādhyakṣa* and *Kaṇṭhakaśhaodhana* courts for hearing the civil and criminal cases. The king encourage the local self government by establishing courts for hearing different cases.

Finance

Vikramāditya managed the administration in such a way that his kingdom became prosperous. His policy in connection with finance was that there was no protection without taxation. The king collected money in different ways without imposing illegal taxation. As a result people became happy with the finance policy of the king.

Sources of revenue to Vikramāditya is known from the inscription of Rudradāmana and Khāraveḷa who were contemporary.

Prisia training was necessary as it is clear from the case of Khāraveḷa. He got education in all branches of learning. Similarly, Rudradāmana and Gautmīputra Sātakarṇī also received training, and they became successful in carrying out the administration. The king promoted welfare activities by constructing roads and other buildings, and opening hospitals.

The foreign affairs between Rudradāmana and Gautamīputra Sātakarṇī are clear from their mutual matrimonial alliances and appointments of ambassadors. Rudradāmana restored the deposed king as it is clear from such examples. Religious toleration policy was adopted by Khāraveḷa and others.

At this time, there were small republics. Among them *Mālavā* republic is the earliest and oldest. The main republics of this region and period were *Mālavās, Yaudheyas, Ārjunāyanas, Śibis, Mādras, Uttamabhadras* etc. There were also republics in neighbourhood. These republics adopted uniform policy in the administration. They had to face foreign invasion and invasion of the powerful kings. Inspite of these, they survived for long time.

SPECIAL FEATURES OF ADMINISTRATION

Vikramāditya adopted the centralised Mauryan policy, besides he introduced policy in the administration. He was also impressed by the political thinkers of his time Khārarveḷa and Rudradāmana. The state was regarded as a welfare state. The king also adopted high ideal of kingship. The king will not do whatever he pleases but what please the people. The king was not only the formal head of the empire but the actual directing head of the Government. The *Saptāṅga* policy of Chandragupta Maurya was continued even by Vikramāditya. The king considered his subjects as son. Vikramāditya also believed that sovereignity is possible only with assistance. A single wheel can never work, hence, the king was helped by the officials. There were territorial units and they were governed by officers. Besides, there were judicial, military, financial and municipal administration. There was espionage system to look after the administration. The earliest *Maṇḍala*-system was followed even now. Such an efficient administration brought great popularity among the masses. The administration at this time was the ideal all around.

It seems that monarchial and republican tribes were ruling at this time. The title *Mahāsenāpati* (Great Commander), after the name fo the ruling chief, shows the military character of the state. An inscription of 226 A.D. discovered at Nāndśā contains the name of *Mahāsenāpati* Nandisome of the Mālavā family, who raised the standard of revolt, probably under the Western Kṣatrapas. In about the first half of the third century A.D., the Maukharīes ruled over the territory of Budva[2] near Kota. *Mahāsenāpati* Bala was at its head in 239 A.D. and he had three grown-up sons to help him in the administration.

The Śakas introduced the Persian type of *Satrapa* government. The title *Kṣatrapa* and *Mahākṣatrapa* show that Western *Kṣatrapas* were originally feudatories of the Kuṣāṇas, but gradually they became independent. The system of joint administration by the king as *Mahākṣatrapa,* with his son of brother, in the junior capacity of *Kṣatrapas* seems to have been a fairly regular practice in the family from the time of Chaṣṭana. In this type of government, the crowned prince, got ample opportunity for training before becoming the ruling chiefs.

Usually, the crown passed on to the eldest son but among the Western *Kṣatrapas,* however, a peculiar mode of succession was established from 200 A.D. and the crown passed from the eldest brother to the younger ones in succession. When the youngest brother died after having his turn to rule, he was succeded by the surviving eldest son of the eldest brother.

REFERENCES

1. Ghoshal, U.N.: *A History of Indian Political Ideas.*
2. *EI*, XXVII, p. 265.
3. *Ibid.*, XXIII, p. 52.

Chapter 10

Religious Conditions

Introduction

Vikramāditya was the follower of Brahmanic religion and this religion was different from such as Śaivism, Vaiṣṇavism and Śaktism. Besides, other minor sects came into existence. Even from the works of Kālidāsa, it seems that there was revival of Vedic religion. Kālidāsa describes sacrifices frequently and in detail. These religious activities created a national awakening among the people in facing the foreign invasions. During this period, Buddhism was adopted by large number of people as known from Sāñchī monuments and inscriptions. As anti-Brahmanical policy, Buddhism still continued near Sāñchī. The comparison of which is not found any where. Jainism became highly developed because of the contributions by Jaina scholars.

Vedic Religion

Vikramāditya made all efforts for the development of Vedic religion, as known from different sources. The

Śuṅgas of Vidīśā tried for its development for performing sacrifices and ritual. and their remains are found. Mādhyamikā and Ujjain were also the centres of Vedic religion. Śakas and Śātavāhanas also tried for the progress of this religion. Vāśavadattā went to Pushkar and performed Vedic rituals. The Nāga rulers of Pawaya also made efforts for its propagation. The republics were advocates of Vedic religion, as known from their coins and inscriptions. The feudal chiefs have established the *Yūpas* for the continuation of the Vedic religion. Sacrifices were performed during this period at various sites, such as Mādhyamikā, Nāndasā 282 (226 A.D.) at Barnala in 228 A.D. and 279 A.D. at Badva in 239 A.D. by *Mahāsenāpati* Bala of the Maukaharīs. Some seals connected with the sacrificial sites have been discovered. These seals have been classified under four heads *viz.* (1) Rulers, (2) Officials, (3)Private individuals and (4) Passport.

Vaiṣṇavism: It was due to the tolerant policy of Vikramāditya that Vaiṣṇavism spread in and outside India. In the last quarter of the second Century B.C., Vaiṣṇavism became a popular religion at Vidīśā. The Besanagar Garuḍa pillar inscription informs that the Garuḍa-staff of Vāsudeva. God of Gods, was erected by Heliodorus who was the Greek ambassdor.

Other Minor Brahmanical Sects: The excavations conducted at Mālavā Nagara, Raidh and Naliāsar give us significant information about anti-activities of the age of Vikramāditya.

Vikramāditya was also the follower of Harsiddhi of Ujjain. It remains and traditions prove it. There still exists more than hundred temples as known from *Avanti Khaṇḍ of Skandapurāṇa* and people worship them. This proves that Vikramāditya had faith in several religions and he was tolerant in religious matters.

The literary works of Kālidāsa and Patañjali, *Mahābhāṣya* give an idea of the religious beliefs prevalent in the society. Brahmanical religions such as Vedic, Śaivism and Vaiṣṇavism were dominant in the society. But it was not the case of Buddhism and Jainism. From other corroborative evidences of coins and literature, it can be advocated that the religion of *Vikramāditya* known as Brahmanical religion was much more popular in the society.

Buddhism

.Buddhism received a setback during the reign of the Śuṅgas who were staunch followers of Brahmanical religions. The successors of Puṣyamitra Śuṇga were tolerant towards Buddhism. It seems that under the Sātavāhanas and Kāṇvas, Buddhism reached its zenith even in the area of Sāñchī during the reign of Vikramāditya.It is also known Vaṣicyaputra Ānanda, the foreman of the artisans of king Sātakarṇī made gift at Sāñchī. Buddhism continued to survive under the Western Kṣatrapa who seems to have recognize the sovereignty of the Kuṣāṇas. From the votive inscription of this period found at Sāñchī, it seems that Buddhism gained footing among the common people of the kingdom of Vikramāditya. The monks, nuns, officers, laymen and laywomen, and the corporate bodies made pious donation to the *Stūpas* of Sāñchī. People of all castes and classes made grants to this holy establishment. Besides individual donations, collective inscriptions were raised particular families, associations and from the inhabitants of particular period. Sāñchī at this time became the place of pilgrimage. People from neighbouring as well as far away places visited it. Devotees from Eran, Māheśvara, Ujjaiyinī etc. were attached with this place. About the end of second century B.C., the Haimavata School of Buddhism became powerful Kosapagota, Dudubhisara and Maihima formed the first group of teachers for the study of Buddhism.

Gautamīputra appears to have held a highly dignified positions in the Buddhist church in Eastern Malwa.

The relics[1] Mahāmogalāna and Sāriputa, the disciples of Buddha, have been enshrined in the Stūpa at Sāñchī and Satadhara in the second century B.C.

The inscribed Buddha and Bodhisattva images of Kuṣāṇa period closely testify that an alien school had already established itself at Sāñchī.

The Buddhist monks, Mataṅga and Dharmarakṣa who belong to Central India, made great efforts for propagation of Buddhism in China in the first century A.D.[2] as known from the translation works.

The age of Vikramāditya from the first Century B.C. to the second century A.D. seems to be peculiar in the history of the world. On one side there was disappearance of Buddhism because of their corrupt practices and on the other side followed ethical practices of some religions and revival of Brahmanism.

Jainism

At the time of Vikramāditya, Jaina scholars propagated Jainism throughout the country. It was the golden age in Jainism. Jaina scholars have written remarkable works during this period. It was the beginning of Śrāvakācāra (Jaina Code of Conduct for house holders) and it simplified the Jaina religion from the rituals. As a result, people easily accepted it.

The great Jaina saint and scholar Kālakācārya lived and propagated Jainism in Avanti during the first century B.C. Some of the Jaina sources claim Vikramāditya as a convert to Jainism.

The Pale (Poona district, Maharashtra) inscription[1] of the first century B.C. commencing with "Namo Arihantānām" proves the existence of Jainism in Maharashtra. The Junagarh inscription of the grandson of Jayadāmana (either Damyasada of Rudrasiṁha I) belonging to the second century A.D. makes a mention of mar who had attained perfect knowledge (Kevala Jñāna) and was free from old age and death (Jaramaraṇa). This inscription contains the earliest reference to Jaina monks claiming the attainment of perfect knowledge.

Jainism appears to have exercised considerable influence over the rulers and the territory of the Sātavāhana dynasty.[4]

According to Jaina traditions, Nahapāna after his defeat at hands of Gautamīputra Sātakarṇī at

Bhṛgukacacha in 66 A.D. became a Jaina monk known as Bhūtabali (C. 66-90 A.D.), after abdicating the throne. Though newly initiated. he might have been considered quite capable for the important task of reediting the Cannons. He was taught by an eminent *Guru* Dharasena, and was guided in his work by his senior colleague Puṣpadanta. He completed the work of *Ṣaṭakhaṇḍā Gama* in century 75 A.D.[5]

The recent excavations[6] in the Krishna valley conducted at *Vaḍḍamaṇu,* identified with the ancient *Vardhamāna* named after the last Jaina Tīrthaṅkara, the name such as *Samprativihāra* and *Jinanavihāra* are found inscribed.

The Jaina teachers like Kundakunda and Sāmantabhadra were reponsible for the diffusion of Jainism in the south. It seems that the original name of Kundakunda was Padmanandī but in course of time, this name was pushed into the background and came to be distinguished more prominently on account of his unique personality by the characterstic name of the place Kundakunda.

Sāmantabhadra, who is known to be the great leader of Jaina religion, lived in the second century A.D. He is known to have gone from place to place for propagation of Jainism and attracted masses.

Jainism also spread much in the second century A.D. by the efforts of Sāmantabhadra who was great Digambara Jaina scholar. According to the "*Śravaṇa Beḷagolā*" inscription dated 1050 Śaka era, he beat the drum (invited literary opponents to refute him) at Pāṭalīputra, in Magadha, in Sindh in Thakka country (the Punjab) and came to Kāñchī in the South and then to Karnataka.[7]

The early migration of Jainas to the country of Kalinga can be seen from the famous Khāravela inscription of Udayagiri dated second or first century B.C. As this inscription refers to the removal of a Jaina image from Kaliṅga to Pāṭalīputra by the Magadha King Nanda. From Magadha to Kaliṅga back, it is proved that Jainism was followed in Kaliṅga in the first and second century B.C. Here the faith took firm root and flourished for a long period. As this inscription starts with invocation (*Maṅgalācharaṇa*) — '*Namo Arihantānām*' and '*Namo-Sava-Siddhanbam*'. Khāraveḷa, the Chedi ruler was the follower of Jainism. He was a zealous patron because he sent missionaries for its propogation. He converted a conference of learned Jainas on the Kumari Hill and consolidated the Aṅgas or sacred texts of Jainism.

As Khāraveḷa was devout Jaina in the South, he was influenced by Vikramāditya and Kaḷkāchārya and other powers of south. He excavated a number of caves in Kumari hill to provide resident to *Arhata* with accomodation and shelter for their bodies. He also constructed cave for the honoured recluse of established reputation as well as for the *Yaties*, hermits and sages hailing from a hundred directions. He also set up many pillars and shrines posts. Though Khāraveḷa was a Jaina, he was tolerant in the matters of religion. The royal epithate सव्व पासडं पूजक attests beyond doubt that king Khāraveḷa observed the principle of religious toleration. Similarly, there would be no necessity for the use of epithate सव्व देवायतन संकार कारके). The repairs of all temples of the deities, there were no worshipper among the people of Kaliṅga of these deities of the temple dedicated to them, Besides Khāraveḷa was the king of religion he was also honourer of every sect.

The Khāraveḷa inscription may be regarded as *Khāraveḷacharita.* It gives more reliable information of the events of his reign and also of the reignal year. We may compare Khāraveḷa with Vikramāditya.

If we rely on coroborative evidence of both Khāraveḷa and Vikramāditya by the names mention in Nanda Dimita of Mathurā, Bṛṣpatimitra of the coin and other evidences, it become clear that Khāraveḷa was contemporary of Vikramāditya.

Religion

Śrāvakācārya, a sect of Jainism. originated during 200 B.C.-300 A.D. the period of Vikramāditya. Its findings, were derived from the Āgama, Śrāvakācārya means house holder having ethical principles, who brought about reforms among the *Saṁghas* of both men and women in many spheres. It is the essence of Jainism, and meant basically for man. It was the greatest contribution to the society. It seems that no religion of the world could stand in comparison with the Śrāvakācāryas. These are against all rituals but followed the principles of Jainism.

REFERENCES

1. *The Mounment of Sanchi,* p. 296.

2. *Chini Buddha dharma kā Itihāsa*, pp. 21-22.
3. *EI*, XXXVIII, pp. 167-168.
4. Desai, P.B., *Jainism in South India and some Jaina Epigraphs, p. 101.*
5. Jain, J.P., *The Jaina Sources of the History of Ancient India (100 B.C.- 900 A.D.)* p. 112.
6. *Arahat Vāchana*, Vol.v, pp. 25, 49-58.
7. Jaina, Hiralal, *Jaina Śilālekha Saṁgarha*, pt. 1, no. 54, p. 102.

Chapter 11

Social Conditions

Introduction

The age of Vikramāditya was important from the part of revolutionary social changes. Vikramāditya was a foresighted person and faced social changes created by new circumstances. He became successful in his policy. Old castes disappeared and new castes were formed. Foreigners like Yavanas, Śakas and Kuṣāṇas etc. were merged into Hindu Society. New social works were written to meet social changes. New society came into exsitence. Inter caste marriages also started at this time. Food and drink habits changed. Wild tribes at this time of Vikramāditya were converted into new caste. The varne system continued to be the basis of social organization.

Divisions of Society

Society was no doubt divided into the usual four *Varṇas*, but mixed marriages, whether among the higher or lower groups, had resulted in the creation of some new castes, such as *Vṛiṣalas*[1], *Varuḍas*[2], *Ugras*[3], *Niṣādas*[4], *Cāṇḍālas*[5] and *Mṛtapas.*[6] Some of these, like the *Vṛiṣalas, Cāṇḍālas* and *Niṣāda,* have been mentioned in Vedic literature. *Varuḍas* belonged to one of the seven low castes called *antyaja,* whose occupation was the splitting of canes. The *Ugra* traced his origin to a Kṣatriya father and a Śūdra mother, and was noted for his cruel disposition and rude conduct. The *Mṛitapas* belonged to that class of persons who took care of the dead, who collected deadmen's clothes, or who excuted criminals. Persons belonging to these groups had an inferior position in the social setting, partly because of their professions, and partly because of their lineage.

Because of the revival of the Brahmanical religion, the status of the Brāhmaṇas increased in society, but emphasis was still laid on their purity. Besides literary and spiritual attainments, they began to follow other profession. Śuṅga and Sātavāhana rulers were Brāhmaṇas by caste. The caste system was rigid and fixed in the society, as seen in one of the inscription of Gautamīputra Śrī Sātakarṇī, who boasts of having prevented the contamination of the four castes and as being the true supporter of the Brāhmaṇas.[7] But a curious fact to note, is that Gautamīputra Sātakarṇī and Rudradāmana were related to each other. Rudradāman, who was a Śaka and of foreign extraction, gave his daughter in marriage to the son of Gautamīputra Sātakarṇī.

At this time, there was a continuous influx of foreigners. Though Hindu society was rigid, it gradually absorbed these foreign elements. The foreigners adopted Hindu names, manners and customs. The son-in-law of Nahapāna bears the Indian name Uṣavadāta, and her daughter's name is Dakṣamitrā. Further, they adopted Brahmanism and Buddhism, and championed them zealously.

A number of sub-castes and *gotras* also came into existence. In the votive inscriptions of Sāñchī, there is mention of *Ḍhamakas, Magalakaṭiyas, Sāphineyakas, Tāpasiyas* and the *Vākhiliyas* of Ujjayinī who made gifts to the Buddhists establishment of Sāñchī[1]. The *goṣṭhi* of the *Barulamisas* of Vidīśā also participated in donations[2]. At Sāñchī, there is mention of a gift by Dharma Rakṣitā of the Mādhava community[10], to *stūpa* I, and gifts from Āryagrāma and Buddha Pālita, the Śreṣṭhī of the race of Pāṇḍu[11] to *stūpa* II.

A ruler named Sarvatāta, who is known from the Ghosuṇḍī inscription,[12] belonged to Gājāyana family. He was the son of a lady of the Pārāśara Gotra. Sogin,[13] Sohartrī[14] and Maukhari[15] seem to be the sub-clans of the Mālavās in the third century A.D.

Family

The family was a homogeneous unit consisting of blood relations, a and the authority of the head of it was recognized. There was a joint family system, because sometimes the donation from a whole family is recorded in the inscription[16] of Sāñchī. They record the family of Dhamu(tara), and the family of Ajitiguṭa. Among the epithets given to *dharāyaṇa* and *Svapnavāsavadattā*, speaks of Ujjayinī, and gives graphic description of its palaces, mansions, temples, gardens, lakes, pleasures, comforts and licenses, which indicate a close contact of the dramatist with the city. U.L. Pusalker[17] places Bhāsa on the fifth or fourth century B.C., but some scholars ascribed him to the second or third century A.D.

Vikramāditya, who is said to have lived in the first century B.C., was a great patron of learning. Under him, Ujjayinī became a synonym for culture. Great poets, dramatists, philosophers, astronomers, scientists and artists flocked to Ujjain. Gaṇaka Kālidāsa, who belonged to 1164 Śaka era, recorded them in the *Jyotirvidābharaṇa.* According to this work, there were nine *Sabhāsads* or court *Paṇḍits* in the court of Vikramāditya. They were Śaṅka, Vararuchi, Maṇi, Aṅgadatta, Jiṣṇu, Trilocana, Hari, Ghaṭakarpara and Amarasiṁha. Besides these there were seven *Kālatantra kavis* or poets conversant with the science of time. Under this head are given the names of Satya, Varāhamihira, Śrutasena, Bādarāyaṇa, Maṇittha and Kumārasiṁha, In addition to these two lists, Gaṇaka Kālidāsa gives a further list of Nine Gems in which the prominent names of the two previous lists are incorporated. The names of nine Gems are :

(1) Dhanavantari
(2) Kṣapaṇaka
(3) Amarasiṁha
(4) Śaṅku
(5) Vetālabhaṭṭa
(6) Ghaṭakarpara
(7) Kālidāsa
(8) Varāhamihira and
(9) Vararuchi.

It is possible that all these great scholars may not have flourished at one and the same time, but it seems that they were attached somehow with Ujjain.

Under the Western Kṣatrapas, Ujjayinī became one of the important seats of learning in India. During this period, Prākṛit was gradually giving place to Sanskrit. The Girnar epigraph is one of the earliest records written throughout in Sanskrit, and displays clearly the existence of an elaborate Sanskrit Literature. It was written in prose, but it also depicts in a most interesting manner, the development from the simple epic to that of the *Kāvya.*[18] Rudradāmana himself was well-versed in Grammar, Politics, Music and Logic. He also seems to have been equally well versed in prose and poetry. The inscriptions of the successors of Rudradāman are also mostly written in Sanskrit. On the contrary, the inscriptions of the contemporary Sātavāhanas are written in Prākṛit, which seems to have been the language of the common folk. The later coins of Dāmaghsada, son of Rudradāmana, are in pure Sanskrit, and the use of Sanskrit legends on the coins was also continued by his son Satyadāmana.[19]

Besides the development of classical Sanskrit literature Levi[20] points out that it was at Ujjayinī, and during the sway of the Śakās, that drama began to develop. Levi[21] points out further, that Śakāra, *i.e.* king's brother-in-law (Śyālaka) of the Sanskrit drama, is in reality a picture of a Śaka, who were Scythian princes ruling for nearly four centuries in Western India. In the drama, Śakāra is a ridiculous figure, a brawling scoundrel, provoking laughter and contempt from the audience.

Such a figure was evidently introduced to bring the alien Śakas into low estimation with the public. The earliest drama in which *'Śakāra'* appears is probably the *'Chārudatta'* of Bhāsa. It is not known what led the great dramatist to bear such a hatred against the Scythians.

Together with the Indian theatre, they must have done a good deal also for the development of Indian musical art, for drama and music are inseparably connected with each other. In the Girnar record, Rudradāmana is credited as having mastered the *Gāndharva vidyā.* Mataṅga, in his *Bṛhaddeśī,* refers to music of foreign extraction, and incidentally mentions *'Śakamiśrita'* and *'Śakākṣya.'* The three branches of this art, *gīta* or music, *vādya* or playing on instruments, and *nṛitya* or dancing, are mentioned by Vātsyāyana, who enjoins that an ideal citizen must be acquainted with at least a rudimentary knowledge of these *kalās.*

It was in Ujjayinī, possibly the capital of the Western Kṣatraps, that Greek astronomy was translated into females in the Sāñchī inscriptions, the repeated occurrence of the old Pāli title *'Pajāvati'*, literally a mother of children, is not without interest, and the fact that some females are named as being merely 'the mother of' and that others proudly proclaim the names of their sons without mentioning their own names, is worthy of note.

Marriage and Position of Women

A lawfully wedded wife is called *'bhāryā'*[22] in the *Mahābhāṣya,* but a synonymous term, *'Ūḍhā'*,[23] is also mentioned. Generally marriages were arranged by parents, who took into consideration the *gotra* and family of the other party. *Sagotra* marriage was not permissible, and one finds references to marital alliances between different *gotras* : the Atri with Bharadvāja, Vaśiṣṭha and Kaśyapa, Bhṛgu and Aṅgirasa, Garga and Bhārgava, and Kutsa and Kuśika.

Women occupied a respectable positon in society. There are many epigraphs as Sāñchī which record gifts from nuns and other ladies. An inscription on the pillar of the *stūpa* at Andher records the gift of Dharma Śiva's mother.[24] It seems that women joined hands with men in the construction of the *stūpas* and gateways. In the sculptures at Sāñchī, women worshipping Buddhist emblems are often depicted in assemblies, playing on instruments, enjoying music and dance, and entertaining guests together with their husbands. That the *Purdā* system did not exist in the society, is known from the sculptures of Sāñchī.

Pastime and Recreations

The pastimes and recreations were many, and were universally enjoyed. Patañjali has mentioned the term '*Samāja*',[25] meaning festive gatherings for which there were numerous items of entertainment, like, music, dancing and acting. Dramatic performances accompanied by music and dancing were arranged. The story of of Kaṁsa and his slaughter, and the binding of Bāli were shown on the stage.[25] In these performances, it was not merely the show, but the speech of the narrator.

and the dialogues, which were enjoyed.[27] The actor used different types of head-dresses.[28] Dancing was also performed, the movements ina rhythmical manner, and the hands expressing themes through gestures. This art is confined to ladies alone. Patañjali refers to female dancers[29], and the Bharhut sculptures show only women dancing. Vocal and instrumental music was common. Certain gestures and postures in the Bharhut sculptures[30] suggest the practice of vocal music. Patañjali has mentioned some musical instruments[31] — drum (*mṛdaṅga*), conch (*śaṅkha)*, flute (*tūṇava)*, and another instrument of the guitar type (*vīṇā*), having seven strings. Wrestling[32], walking[33] and fire displays[34] were other recreations. The indoor recreations included the game of dice[35] which was probab;y meant for the old and rich, who had the time and money to do so.

Food and Drinks

Patañjali[36] gives exhaustive information about food and drinks, with vegetarian and non-vegetarian items, solid and liquid food, arrangements for meals, milk preparations, sweets, wines and fruits, and even dinner etiquette. Rice, wheat barley and pulses are used by the people. The sweet balls popularly known as *Modaka* were liked by children. Generally, the meat of deer, goat, sheep, and the *sāraṅga* bird, was popular. Different kinds of drinks, both soft and alcholic, were enjoyed.

Dress and Ornaments

Some literary works, the sculptural representations

of Sāñchī, and some figures of Yakṣa and Yakṣī, gave us some idea of the dress and ornaments of the people. The lower garment was called '*upasaṁvyāna*'[37], corresponding to the modern *dhotī*-loin, which was genreally white. The upper cloth for covering shoulders, was called *paṭa.*[38] Patañjali also refers to the use of cotton[39] and wool[40]. Clothes were sewn with a sharp needle.[41] Patañjali refers to leather shoes as well as to wodden sandals.[42] Women wore a skirt, generally white in colour[43]. The dyeing of clothes was very common. Patañjali[44] has referred to blue (*nīla),* yellow (*pīta*), green (*harit*) and brown red (*kāṣāya*) colours.

The Yakṣa figure of Besanagar of this period, wears a *dhotī* tied with a heavy waist band, and the upper part of the body is carved with *uttarīya.* The dress of the Yakṣa, Maṇibhadra of Pawaya, consists of waist-cloth and a scarf. From the study of the sculptures of Sāñchī, we know that both men and women used upper and lower garments. The head dress for men was generally of *śaṁkhākāra* (shape of conch) fashion. On rare occassions, women put on the lower garments in '*Sakaccha*' fashion, *i.e.* by passing one end of it between the legs and tucking it up behind at the waist. The cloth was fastened at the waist by a girdle. Soldiers, body-guards, charioteers (*sārathī*), standard-bearers (*dhvajavāhaka*), Brāhmaṇas and saints put on their own peculiar dress.

The Scythians are represented as wearing trousers and big overcoats, and this was immitated by the Indians. Women too began to wear blouses, jackets and frocks, in immtation of the Greeks and the Scythians, but the fashion did not become a general one.

Patañjali[45] mentions four kinds of ornaments *ruchaka* (necklace), *kaṭaka* (bracelet), *svastika* (triangular piece), and *kuṇḍala* (ear-ring). Both men and women wore these ornaments. The forehead pieces like *latika* or the fastened leaf, long collars, garlands, zones or girdles, and anklets, were exclusively meant for women. The Yakṣī figure of Besanagar wears ornaments like necklaces, ear-rings, armelts and wristlets. She has a heavy nine-beaded *mekhalā* on her waist. The ornaments on the Yakṣa Maṇibhadra of Pawaya, comprise of rich neklace, consisting of a number of jewel or pearls strings, knotted and hanging down in tassels on the back, an armlet on the right arm, and bracelet on the left-wrist. There was a plain, nimbus round the head, which has left its traces on both sides of the neck. An idea of these ornaments is also gained from the sculptures of Sāñchī. Rings, ear-rings, strings of beads, gridles of beads, bangles. necklaces, braclets made of gold, silver, copper and ivory, have been discovered in the excavtion of old sites..

The figures at Bhārhut and Sāñchī, show different methods of arranging the hair. The loose hair is allowed to fall at the back, and then the end is looped and knotted.[46] It is arranged in a top-knot when the lady has a head dress.[47] The hair falling down the back is divided into two halves, and that into tassels, and then plaited[48], Men generally had long hair tied in a top-knot, around, which the fold of the turbans were arranged.[49] The fashion of plaited hair, of the women, coiled around the head in a top knot, is also observed in sculptures.[50] In some cases, the hair is fastened by an ornament.[51] Curly locks touching the neck are favoured by musicians, charioteers, and soldiers.[52] The arranging of hair needed oil, combs and mirrors, while collyrium sticks, unguent vases and pots, were required for the make-up of the face. Patañjali mentions *chandana*-sandal, *gandha*-perfume, and *añjana* or black pigment appllied to the eye lashes.

Names of persons were kept in different ways. From some votive inscriptions of Sāñchī, it is known that a considerable group of proper names, *e.g. Asāḍa, Mūla, Mūladatā, Phaguṇa, Poṭhak, Pusa, Pusaka, Pusani, Pusagiri, Purasakhita, Pothādevā, Rohiṇī, Sātila,* and *Svatiguṭa,* have been derived from the names of the *Nakṣatras,* and point to the conclusion that the rule of some *Gṛhyasūtras,* which recommends the use of *Nakṣatranāmānī,* was observed.

REFERENCES

1. Patañjali *Mahābhāṣya* - I.1.7, p. 59, l.18.
2. *Ibid.,* IV, I.97, p. 253. l.5
3. *Ibid.,* IV, I.14, p. 257, l.15.
4. *Ibid.,* V, 4.36, p. 435, l.8.
5. *Ibid.,* II.4.10, p. 475, l.6.
6. *Ibid.*
7. EI,VIII, p. 71.
8. *The Monument of Sāñchī,* p. 297.
9. *Ibid.*
10. *CBT,* p. 152.
11. *Ibid.,* p. 180.
12. *EI,* XVI, p. 27.
13. *Ibid,* XXVII, pp. 252.

14. *Ibid.*, XXVII, pp. 118.
15. *The Guhilas fo Kiṣkindhā.* p. 42.
16. *EI*, II, p. 87 f.
17. *Bhāsa — A Study.*
18. Keith : *A history fo Sanskrit Literature*, p. 49.
19. Rapson; *Catalogue*, p. 82.
20. *JA*, 1902, pp. 95-125.
21. *Le Theatre Indian*, p. 361.
22. IV. I52, p. 22, l.17.
23. *Ibid.*, I.1.1, p. 42, l. 16.
24. *CBT*, p. 222.
25. Patañjali *Mahābhāṣya*, I, 1, 50, p. 123, l. 3.
26. *Ibid.*, III. 1.26, p. 36, l.15.
27. *Ibid.*, I,4,26, p. 329 l.8.
28. *Ibid.*, II.1.69, p. 403, l.8.
29. *Ibid.*, VI.3.42, p. 158, l.16.
30. Barua : Bharhut fig. 34, 69, 136.
31. Patañjali, II.2.34, p. 435, l.11.
32. *Ibid.*, III.4.47, p. 181, l.18.
33. *Ibid.*, VIII.1, 7, p. 370, l.1.
34. *Ibid.*, III.2.124, p. 125, l.17.
35. *Ibid.*, I.4.2, p. 310, l.4.
36. Patañjali, *Mahābhāṣya*,
37. *Ibid.*, 1,1,36, p. 93, l.12.
38. *Ibid.*, 1.4.21, p. 321,l.16.
39. *Ibid.*, IV.1.55, p. 224, l.14.
40. *Ibid.*, V.1.3, p. 338, l.19.
41. *Ibid.*, II.12, p. 373, l.20.
42. *Ibid.*, V.1.2, p. 337, ll.6-7.
43. *Ibid.*, II.2.5, p. 410, l.21.
44. *Ibid.*, IV.2.2, p. 271. l.10.f.
45. *Ibid.*, I,1,I, p.7, l.15f.

46. Barua, Bharhut, vol., III, p. XXIII-top.
47. *Ibid.*, pl. XXX, 23, left side.
48. *Ibid.*, pl. XXXIX, 34.
49. *Ibid.*, III, pl. XXX, 23.
50. Ferfusson, *Trees and Serpent Worship*, Pl. XXX, fig.1. XXXII fig. 2.
51. *Ibid.*, pl. XXXV, fig. 2.
52. *Ibid.*, pl, XXXIV, fig. 1.22.

Chapter 12

Economic Conditions

Introduction

The age of Vikramāditya was also important from economic point of view. The kingdom of Vikramāditya established during this period gradually became rich. A large number of coins of different types were discovered. This shows the prosperity of the region. Because of convenient communication, trade and commerce developed. Trade with foreign countries also started. Merchants occupied important position because of their wealth. Economically this region became prosperous. There was also increased agriculture production and mines were noticed. In this way, the economic progress led to the golden age.

Economic Conditions

There was ample production of raw material in Avanti. The case of communications during this period led to the development of trade, both internal and external. A large number of professions came into existence, which were organised into guilds. The prosperity of this region is also evident from the fact that most of the donors who built the *stūpas* at Sāñchī and in the neighbourhood, came from this area.

This region produced an abundance of cotton. The village of Kāpāsigāmā[1], mentioned in three inscribed labels on the railing of Sāñchī *stūpa* I, is a proof of its vast production, because the village was named after it, Cotton industries must have been flourshing at important cities, such as Ujjain and Vidiśā. In fact, the region was famous for the export of fine muslins.

The area was rich in quarries, as is clear from their findings at different excavations. It is for this reason that the region was known as Ākarāvanti in the second century A.D., is known from the Girnar inscription[2] of Rudradāmana. It may be inferred from the account of the commercial importance of Uzene in the *Periplus,* that Avanti was a country which abounded in quarries of stones like onyx.

The iron industry was also gradually developing. On examination a specimen of some metal wedges used at the bottom of the *Garuḍa* pillar of Besanagar, Robert Hatfield, an authority on steel in England, proved that it was of real steel.[3] Thus Avanti knew the process of steel-making as early as the second century B.C. This was an important fact in the future economic progress of the province.

Communication was smooth and frequent, as seen in the benefactions at Sāñchī made by persons coming from different parts of India. This must have given impetus to internal trade. In Avanti, the three routes from the western coast met, from the sea-ports Surpāraka (Sopara) and Bhṛgukaccha (Broach), from the Deccan and from Śrāvastī. It seems that there was a brisk trade with the two important marts, namely Paithana and Tagara in the Deccan. It was also carried on with the important trade centres of the Gangetic valley. Avanti exported its main products, such as onyx-stones, cotton and grains.

Trade was not only internal, but also external. The unknown author of the '*Periplus*' of the Erythraean Sea, of the second half of the first century A.D., gives information about the external trade. Merchandise from Ujjain and other remote places in the north, were brought to Bhṛgukaccha for export to foreign countries. The chief articles were onyxstones, porcelain, fine muslins, mallow tinted cotton etc.

As a result of commercial and industrial development, a large number of professions and crafts came into existence. Some are mentioned in the votive inscriptions[4] of Sāñchī, such as Sotika, *i.e. Sautrika* (weaver), *vaḍaki, i.e. Vardhakin* (carpenter) and *daṁtakāra* (worker in ivory). Besides these, there were hunters, trappers, fishermen, butchers and tanners. Their existence is proved by the manufactured objects unearthed in the archaeological excavations.

Some of the crafts and industries were organized into guilds. The guild of the ivory workers of Vidiśā was well known, and it made a gift to the *stūpa* at

Sāñchī. The foreman of the artisans was known as *āvasenī* and his name is mentioned in the inscription at Sāñchī[1] The head of the merchant guild was known as *śreṣṭhī* who is frequently mentioned in the votive inscription of Sāñchī.

Coinage

During this period, punch-marked coins, and Ujjaiyinī coins continued for some time, but gradually, they were replaced by other coins. In form character, and standard of weight, they were influenced by the Graeco-Bactrian and Roman coins. This was inevitable, because of the trade and commerce with the west. Even foreign names like *dīnāra* and *dramma* were applied to them. Yet in spite of the foreign influence, some elements of the early coinage were retained.

The Śaka silver coins have the bust of the king together with meaningless traces of circular Greek legend, borrowed from the Indo-Bactrian prototype on the obverse. The circular Brāhmī legend on the reverse of these coins, carefully mentions the name and the title, not only of the ruler, but also of his father. From the reign of Jīvadāman (175 A.D.), each coin issued from the mint borne the date. The cresented three-arched hill with the sun and the moon on either side, is the reverse symbol on the Kṣatrapa coins. In course of time, the hill in the centre dominated the other two, which dwindled into insignificance. The average weight of the silver coins of the Western Kṣtrapas is about thirty-five grains. They are obviously hemidrachms of the Persian weight standard.

The lead, potin and copper coins of the Western Kṣatrapas have been found in abundance in the Ujjain-Bhilsa region. One silver coin of Chaṣṭana as Mahākṣatrapa, was found at Ujjain[6]. On the obverse, there is a bust of the king with the traces fo Greek legend. On the reverse, there is a *chaitya* of six-arches surmounted by a rayed Sun on the left, and a crescent on the right. Coins with the figures of bulls are also found in this area. Potin coins of the Western Kṣatrapas having on the obverse the figure of an elephant and on the reverse a *chaitya,* seem to be restricted to this area.

A hoard of Kṣtatrapa coins was found during the excavations at Sāñchī. Another hoard of fifty-one silver coins of the Western Kṣtrapas was obtained from Gonderman[7] eleven kilometers north-west of Bhopal. The hoard consisted of five coins of the Mahākṣatrapa Vijayasena, six coins of the Mahākṣatrapa Rudrasena II, seventeen coins of Bhartṛdāman both as Kṣatrapas and Mahākṣatrapa, ten coins of the Kṣatrapa Viśvasena, three coins of the Kṣatrapa Rudrasiṁha II, and one coin of the Mahākṣatrapa Svāmī-Rudrasena III. The attribution of the remaining nine coins is uncertain. All the coins were dated, the legible dates ranging from Śaka 157 to 270 (235 A.D. to 348). Like the Uparkot and Sarvaniā hoards, this hoard appears to have been buried at the end of the earlier reign-period of the Mahākṣatrapa Svāmī Rudrasena III, whose coins are the latest to be represented.

The Sātavāhana ruler issued their own distinctive coinage, with the hill and the Ujjain symbol as permanent features. There are metronymics together with personal names in Brāhmī. These are of lead, potin, copper and silver.

Early coins in lead and potin have been found with the legend '*Rāño Siri Sātasa.*' On the obverse, there is a figure of an elephant, and the symbological representation of a river with fishes, and on the reverse, there is the Ujjaiyinī symbol. These coins may be attributed to the Mālavā region from the consideration of their type.[8]

After capturing this Malwa region from the Śaka ruler Nahapāna, Gautamīputra Sātakarṇī counterstruck his silver coins. On these, there is the *chaitya* of three arches on the obverse, and the Ujjaiyinī symbol on the reverse. He also issued the coin type which were already current in this region, such as the homo-figure, the Elephant and the Lion, and the *Svastika* between the taurine symbols. His son, Vāśiṣṭhīputra Pulumāvī, began the practice of issuing silver coins with the royal portrait. His successors, Vāśiṣṭhīputra Sātakarṇī and Yajñaśrī Sātakarṇi, continued it,

At Pawāyā in the first or second century A.D. symbolic types of coins were current.[9] These coins are triangular in shape with the symbols of a triangle, a Sun, a monkey, a Nāga, a tree within a railing, a trident, a lion standing, a bull walking etc. On the early coins of this area, the names of the rulers such as Amitasena, Sabalasena, Yagata, etc.[10] are inscribed.

In the third and fourth centuries A.D. the Nāga coins, which are similar to Mālavā coins in fabric, were issued in the regions of Pawaya (Padmāvatī) and Kutwar (Kāntipuri)[11]. These coins are die-struck. Most of them are round, but some are rectangular. On one side of the coins, there is a symbol in a circle of pellets, one group bearing the figure of a peacock, and the other of a humped bull. Some of the Nāga rulers issued coins with an additional recurring symbol. These symbols are – a trident, a crescent, a lion and a wheel. Excepting the last one, all are Śaivite emblems. The other side has a fragmentary Brāhmī legends — *Mahārāja, Adhirāja* and *Śrī*. These are of copper and conform to the standard of thirty six, eighteen and nine grains, representing a *kākiṇī*, a half *kākiṇī*, and a quarter *kākiṇī* respectively.

REFERENCES

1. *CBT*, p. 160, no. 99.
2. *EI*, VIII, pp. 42 ff.
3. *Vikrama Volume* (Eng. Ed.), p. 378, f.n.1.
4. *EI*, II, pp. 87f.
5. *Ibid.*
6. *JNSI*, XIV, p. 20.
7. *IAR*, 1953-54, p. 63.
8. Rapson, *Catalogue of the Indian Coins in the British Museum*, p. xcii,
9. *JNSI*, XVIII, part I, p. 67, part II, p. 163.
10. *Ibid.*, xvii, p. 53.
11. *Catalogue of the Coins of the Nāga kings of Padmāvati.*

Chapter 13

Art and Architecture

Introduction

Most of the art specimen of the age of Vikramāditya have been lost but those survived give an idea of that art. For this purpose we shall study the time and region of the art. This art had its own peculiar features and it was influenced by the foreigners like Greeks, Śakas and Kuṣāṇas. This art seems to have originated independently. Vikramāditya seems to be the patron of this art. The great religious movement of the time of Vikramāditya gave an impetus to the art and architecture of this region. This art prosperity led to the development of different aspects. Ujjain was just like heaven on the earth, because of the development of different spheres made by Vikramāditya. The art of Vikramāditya may be divided under the following categories :

1. Religious architecture.
2. Secular art and architecture.
3. Minor Arts.

Religious Architecture

The earliest known Jaina image is from the Jaina temple of Lohanipura near Patna from which two torsos of Jaina image were found, Nigatasa Vihāra Dipe inscribed on one of the pot shreds at Kasrawad in Madhya Pradesh proves the existence of Jaina monastery in the third century B.C. The excavations conducted at a site called Vaddamanu named after Vardhamana in the Krishna valley, yielded the Jaina remains of the *stūpas* ellipsoidal structures and monastries of the period between the second century B.C. to the second century A.D. The names Jinonavihāra and *Sampratīvihāra* are found engraved on the pottery. The name Samprativihāra proves that Samprati was a historical figure.

The religious architecture consisted of *stūpas, vihāras* and temples. Those discovered give an idea of the architecture of this period. Sāñchī remained religious place in the first century B.C. The four elaborately richly carved gateways were built in the four directions of the *stūpa*. In size and construction, *stūpa* second was almost replica of *stūpa* first. The main difference was the decoration of the ground railing. *Stūpa* third is smaller in size and the ground railing has almost entirely disappeared. There was stairway with balustrade similar to that of *stūpa* first, in style decoration and structural form. The apsidal temple number eighteen belong to Śuṅga age, and its plan is similar to that of the rock cut temple of Karli. Outside the town of Besanagar, remains of the *stūpa* of this period have been discovered. Even at Udayagiri, the remains of the Buddhist *stūpa* and monuments in the neighbourhood of Sāñchī such as Sonari, Satadharā, Bhojpur and Andher, have been found. Besides Sāñchī, Buddhist monuments have been found at Ujjain and Kasaravada.

Jaina architecture in the Khandgiri caves of Khāraveḷa and the caves of Udayagiri give an idea of cave-architecture. There were Jaina temples in Mathurā and remains of Jaina architecture at Ujjain of Avanti Sukumal temple. In temples of this period we find *prakāra* and roof base Nagar and Nagari. There were remains of the *Yūpa* and also there are remains of temples both in Besanagar and Nagri. These were the Vaiṣṇava temples. Mahākāla temple of Ujjain was the oldest Śhiva temple. Its existence is known from the Śivaliṅga and bull symbol are even found on coins.

Buddhist Sculptures

The sculptures of the four gateways with their architraves and pillars of the first stupa on the balustrade of the second *stūpa,* the base reliefs relate to Buddha's life showing his birth, enlightenment and death. During this period sculptured art became narrative which have been illustrated beside historical scenes such as the visit of Ajatāśatru and Prasannajīt of Kośala, figures of animals or birds are also found. There are also female figures.

Brahmanical Sculputres

There are also sculptures of human beings such as Yakṣas, Devatās, Nāgas and Apsarās. The statue of Yakṣas and Yakṣies are found at Besanagar. Some statues of Nāgas and Nāgins, both in human form, are found in Vidiśā. Some sculptures of Buddha and Bodhisattvas of the Kuṣaṇa's period were discovered at Sāñchī. The early image of Balarāma found at Tumain is interesting from the artistic point of view.

We have the earliest remains of the structural shrine at Bairot that goes back to the third century B.C.[1] The Pujasilaprakara mentioned in the inscription of the second century B.C. at Nagari proves the earliest trace of the existence of Vaiṣnava temple. Two things were erected in Nārāyaṇa vāṭikā. One is *śilapaṭa* for the worship and another the surrounding wall. *Śilapaṭa* was on the platform, which was surrounded by the walls.[2]

Secular Architecture

The excavated site such as Ujjain, Mālavā, Nagar, Besanagar etc. revealed about the fortification wall with moat and gates. An idea of secular architecture is gained from the study of the residential buildings discovered in the excavations, besides following the earlier tradition of having foundations of course rubbles. People introduced the use of foundation. The brick foundation may be traced in this period, a number of brick construction appear to be the remains of sculptures belonging to this period. At Ramagarh, there are two caves. Sitabenga and Jogimera. There is suitable arrangements for the ampi theatre whcih speaks of Ujjayinī, and gives graphic description of its places, mansions, temples, gardens, lakes, pleasures and comforts. It indicates a close contact of the dramatist with the city.

Jaina Sculptures

Jaina sculptures of Jaina Tīrthaṅkaras and Jaina dieties Sarasvatī, Ambikā of the Kuṣāṇa period have been discovered. Jaina sculptures are found in *Padmāsana* and *Kāyotsarga*. Besides the symbols of of individual *tīrthaṅkara*, there are some other symbols also found in Jaina images. From the point of view of art, these are artistic.

Terracottas

Some ancient sites such as Ujjain, Eran, Maheshwar, Besanagar, Awara, Tumain and Sodang, yielded a large number of terracottas. These are of different varieties, and serve different purposes. Decoration of house, objects of worship, play objects for children and magical and totemic objects. The cult of mother goddess continued during this period as it is clear from their terracottas unearthed at different sites. Some terracottas of human figure were discovered at Tumain, Besnagar and Awara. Among the animal figures those of the bull, are the most important at Dangawada, Sodang and Awara.

Pottery

This period is marked by the disappearance of the north black polished ware but black and red ware continued. This period in later phase is characterized by red polished ware, found extensively in excavated sites. The Roman Samian ware was due to the foreign contact for commercial use. This pottery became very popular, it was imported from the Mediteranean. Besides Madhya

Pradesh, these were available at site in Gujarat, Rajasthan and in Maharashtra. The forms of the vessels of this pottery are dishes, bowls, beakers, cups etc.

Minor Arts

Among the minor arts of this period, the jewellers occupied a prominent place. The base reliefs at Sāñchī throw light on the ornaments of the people. The images of Yakṣa and Yakṣi and of Maṇibhadra of Pawāyā ivory was used. Other kinds of ornaments were ear-rings, bracelets, anklets, and girdles etc.

REFERENCES

1. *EI*, XXII, p. 204.
2. *Ibid.*, XII. p. 531.

Chapter 14

Education, Literature and Sciences

Introduction

Ujjayinī became a great seat of learning because of the existence of the *Āśrama* of Sāndīpani in the second century B.C. There were tradtions at that time that it was founded by the ancient *Ṛshi* Sāndīpani, who was the tutor of Śrīkṛiṣṇa and Balarāma. Such was the name and fame of this institution, that students from distant places came for higher studies. The subjects taught were the *Vedas, Dharmaśāstra,* Religion, Philosophy, *Nītiśāstra,* Accountancy, and Archery, etc. The students lived under the guidance of their teachers, and they led a celibate life. They served their teachers by performing several duties. Some *Purāṇas* and other literary works also, describe this ancient educational institution of Ujjain.[1]

Education

Patañjali whose traditional birthplace was Gonarda[2] in Avanti, indirectly refers to the prevalent educational system in his *Mahābhāṣya.* Emphasis was laid on the study of Grammar which was necessary for the preservation of the *Vedas.*[3] Besides Grammar, the other subjects of study were four *Vedas,* with six *Aṅgas,* their mysteries, a hundred *śākhās* of *Yajur-veda,* and the *Sāma-veda* with its thousand *pāṭhas,* treatises on dialogue, or the science of Logic, Epic, *Purāṇas* and Medicine[4]. Other studies included *Saṁgraha,* Metrics,[5] *Dharmaśāstra*[6], Astrology[7] and a comparative study of all doctrines (*Sarva-tantra*)[8], and popular subjects like the tales of *Sumanottarā* and *Vāsavadattā.*[9] The *Smṛtis,* Chiromancy and the science of animals are also mentioned.

Patañjali refers to *gurukula* or the 'teacher's house' where the pupils lived under the guidance of the preceptor.[10] The boarders were known as '*ante-vāsin*'[11] and the teacher providing lodging was called '*anteguru*'[12] Generally, the relations between the preceptor and his pupils were very cordial. With begging bowl in his hands, the pupil went out on rounds[13] to the householders for food and other necessities.[14]

The method of the study was the rote system, but there was scope for discussion and interpretation for a proper understanding of the texts. Emphasis was laid on pronunciation and recitation. Despite insistence on rote method, writing was in use. It is certain that Greek, *Kharoṣṭhī,* and *Brāhmī,* were popular scripts in that period.

Patañjali also refers to female education. According to him, terms *Upādhyāyā* and *Upādhyāyī*[15] denoted a female teacher. He also mentions a young girl of the *Aupagavī* school[16], and a Brāhmaṇī studying *Kāsakṛtsnī* doctrines.[17]

There was *Pariṣad*[18] of the learned persons who knew the *Vedas,* the *Dharmas* and the sciences. It appears that it regulated the academic activities of different groups or schools, and served as a means for the development and propagation of learning. The pupils were known after the *gotras* and the *chāraṇas* of the teachers.

The question of fees, it seems, was not very important, because the diffusion of learning had no mercenary motive. It was the duty of the householders to meet the requirements of the preceptor and his family, as well as his pupils. The students were expected to pay fees in cash or in kind, so that the teacher could maintain himself and his family.

Literature

This period is noteworthy for the revival of Sanskrit literature and literary creation. Patañjali, the great Grammarian, author of the *Mahābhāṣya,* lived in this period. He was probably the chief priest in the *yajña* performed by Puṣyamitra Śuṅga.

Ujjayinī became a great centre of learning. and it attracted a large number of scholars. Rājaśekhara[19] records a tradition the Viśālā was an examination center where poets used to be examined. It is said that Kālidāsa, Meṇṭha, Amara, Rūpa, Sūra, Bhāravi, Hariścandra and Chandragupta were examined at Ujjain. However, about the period in which these writers flourished nothing can be definitely stated.

Bhāsa in his plays *Avimāraka, Cārudatta, Pratijñā-*

Yaugandharāyaṇa and *Svapnavāsavadatta*, speaks of Ujjayinī, and gives graphic description of its palaces, mansions, temples, gardens, lakes, pleasure, comforts and licenses, which indicate a close contact of the dramatist with the city U.L. Pusalkar[20] places Bhāsa in the fifth or fourth century B.C., but some scholars ascribed him to the second or third century A.D.

Vikramāditya, who is said to have lived in the first century B.C., was a great patron of learning. Under him, Ujjayinī became a synonym for culture, Great poets, dramatists, philosophers, astronomers, scientists and artists flocked to Ujjain. Gaṇaka Kālidāsa, who belonged to 1164 Śaka era, recorded them in *Jyotirvidābharaṇa*. According to this work, there were nine *Sabhāsads* or court *Paṇḍits* in the court of Vikramāditya. They were Śaṅka, Vararuchi, Maṇi, Aṅgadatta, Jiṣṇu, Trilochana, Hari, Ghaṭakarpara and Amarasiṁha. Besides these, there were seven *Kālatantra kavis* or poets conversant with the science of time. Under this head are given the names of Satya, Varāhamihira, Śrutasena, Bādarāyaṇa, Maṇittha and Kumārasiṁha. In additon to these two lists, Gaṇaka Kālidāsa gives a further list of Nine Gems in which the prominent names of the two previous lists are incorporated. The names of nine Gems are: (1) Dhanvantari, (2) Kṣapaṇaka, (3) Amarasiṁha, (4) Śaṅku, (5) Vetālabhaṭṭa, (6) Ghaṭakarpara, (7) Kālidāsa, (8) Varāhamihira and (9) Vararuchi. It is possible that all these great scholars may not have flourished at one and the same time, but its seems that they were attached somehow with Ujjain.

Under the Western Kṣatrapas, Ujjayinī became one of the important seats of learning in India. During this period, Prākṛit was gradually giving place to Sanskrit. The Girnar epigarph is one of the earliest records written throughout in Sanskrit, and displays clearly the existence of an elaborate Sanskrit Literature. It was written in prose, but it also depicts in a most interesting manner, the development from the simple epic to that of the *Kāvya*,[21] Rudradāmana himself was well-versed in Graṃmar, Politics, Music and Logic. He also seems to have been equally well versed in prose and poetry. The inscriptions of the successors of Rudradāmana are mostly written in Sanskrit. On the contrary, the inscriptions of the contemporary Sātavāhanas are written in Prākṛit, which seems to have been the language of the common folk. The later coins of Dāmaghsada, son of Rudradāmana, are in pure Sanskrit, and the use of Sanskrit legends on the coins was also continued by his son Satyadāmana.[22]

Besides the development of classical Sanskrit literature, Levi[23] points out that it was at Ujjayinī, and during the sway of the Śakas, that drama began to develop. Levi[24] points out further, that Śakāra, *i.e.* king's brother-in-law (Śyālaka) of the Sanskrit drama, is in reality a picture of a Śaka, who were Scythian princes ruling for nearly four centuries in Western India. In the drama, Śakāra is a ridiculous figure, a brawling scoundrel, provoking laughter and contempt from the audience. Such a figure was evidently introduced to bring the alien Śakas into low estimation with the public. The earliest drama in which '*Śakāra*' appears is probably the

'*Chārudatta*' of Bhāsa. It is not known what led the great dramatist to bear such hatred against the Scythians.

Together with the Indian theatre, they must have done a good deal also for the development of Indian musical art, for drama and music are inseparably connected with each other. In the Girnar record, Rudradāmana is credited as having mastered the *Gāndharva vidyā*. Mataṅga, in his *Bṛhaddeśī*, refers to music of foreign extraction, and incidentally mentions '*Śakamiśrita*' and '*Śakākshya*'. The three branches of this art, *gīta* or music, *vādya* or playing on instruments, and *nṛetya* or dancing, are mentioned by Vātsyāyana, who enjoins that an ideal citizen must be acquainted with at least a rudimentary knowledge of these *kalās*.

It was in Ujjaiyinī, possibly the capital of the Western Kṣtatrapas, that Greek astronomy was translated into Indian soil, which was ultimately recast and remodelled by the Indians.

Sciences

Sciences made striking progress during the first and second century A.D. because of contact with the Western World. Ujjain became a great centre not only of trade but also of scientific knowledge. Bhāsa, the Sanskrit dramatist, refers to the observatory of Ujjain where records were taken of the Sun. It was in Ujjaiyinī possibly the capital of the Western Kṣatrapas, that Greek astronomy was translated into Indian soil, which was ultimately recast and remodelled by the Indians. As Kālidāsa was somehow associated with Ujjain, it was but natural that he possessed knowledge of different sciences such as Astronomy, Mathematics, Medicines and Chemistry.

REFERENCES

1. *Brahmāṇḍa-purāṇa. Padmapurāṇa, Viṣṇupurāṇa, and Bhāgavata.*
2. IHQ, 1926, 267. According to the *Sutta Nipāta,* Gonarda stood mid-way between Ujjain and Besanagar.
3. Patañjali's *Mahābhāṣya,* 1.1.1, p. 1. l.15.
4. *Ibid.*, I.1.1, p. 9 ll.21-23.
5. *Ibid.*, I.2.32, p. 208. l.19.
6. *Ibid.*, I.2.64, p. 242. l.25.
7. *Ibid.*, VI.3.79, p. 170. l.17.
8. *Ibid.*, IV. 2.60, p. 284. l,12.
9. *Ibid.*, IV. 2.60, p. 284. l,12.
10. *Ibid.*, IV. 2.62, p. 333. l,1.
11. *Ibid.*, IV. 3.104, p. 315. l.22.
12. *Ibid.*, IV. 3.10, p. 145. l.16.
13. *Ibid.*, I.4.84, p. 347, l.17.
14. *Ibid.*, I.1.55, p. 133. l.25.
15. *Ibid.*, III.3.21, p. 147. l.20.
16. *Ibid.*, IV.1.93, p. 247. l.24.
17. *Ibid.*, IV. 1.14, p. 206. l.9.
18. *Ibid.*, III.3.108, p. 155. l.10.
19. *Kāvyamīmāṁsā,* 3rd., ed. p. 55.
20. Bhāsa — *A study.*
21. Keith : *A History fo Sanskrit Literature,* p. 49.
22. Rapson : *Catalogue,* p. 82.
23. *JA*, 1902, pp. 95-125.
24. *Le Theatre Indian,* p. 361.

Chapter 15

Vikramāditya and His Subjects

For the first time, we have mentioned here the works and their authors which are as follows :

(1) *Charitra-Prabhṛta* of Kundakunda, (2) *Tattvārtha sūtra* of Umāsvāmin, (3) *Ratnakarandaka* of Samantabhadra, (4) *Upāsakadhyayana* of Somadeva, (5) *Puruṣārtha siddhyupaya* of Amṛtachandra.

The religious, social and other type of services rendered, are as follows:

(1) Śrāvaka and Śrāvakāchāra, (Samyaktva, the Mūlagaṇas, the Vratas, the Anu-Vratas, the Guṇa-Vratas, Śikṣā Vratas, and the Aticāras).

(2) The Anu-Vratas (the Ahiṁsānu-Vrata, the Satyānu-Vratas, the Ācāuryanu-Vrata, the Brahmacaryanu-Vrata, the Parigraha-Parimāṇa Vrata, and Ratri-bhojana).

(3) The Guṇa-Vrata and Śikṣā Vratas (the Dig-Vrata, the Deśa-Vrata, the *Anārtha-daṇḍa-Vrata,* the *Sāmayika-Vrata,* the *Prasadhapavasa-Vrata,* the *Bhogopabhoga-*

Parimāṇṇa-Vrata, the Dāna-Vrata and the Sallekhanā-Vrata).

Significance of Śrāvakachara

1. Ethical discipline in Jainism, the layman Doctrine.
2. *Jaina Saṅgha* — an ideal social organization.
3. *Samyagdarshan* — the right faith.
4. *Aṣṭa-Mūla-Guṇas* — the eight basic virtues.
5. The twelve Vows, the five smaller ones and the principle of *Ahiṁsā*.
6. The house holder's or Layman's *Ahiṁsā* — non-violence.
7. Peculiarities of the Vows of *Satya*-Truthfulness, *Ācārya*-non-stealing and *Brahmacharya* – sexual morality.
8. Guṇa-Vratas – the strengthening Rules of conduct.
9. Śikṣā-Vratas — the Disciplinary Rules of conduct and the Role *Dāna*–Charity.
10. The Role of *Pūjā* — Worshipping.
11. *Sallekhanā* — Willing submission to the inevitable death.

Vikramāditya and Śrāvakas (Householder) *Śrāvaka Dharma* or *Śrāvakācāra*, a sort of Jaina religion developed from the first century B.C and second century A.D. in different parts of the country. The greatest contribution of this religion is that it reformed the society and removed the evils. It was dependent on basic principles of life. The credit for the propagation of this religion goes to monks who moved from place to place and to authors who wrote several works on this religion. This work seems to have been derived from the Āgamas.

Śrāvaka Dharma was named after the Śrāvaka. Originally, Śrāvakas and Śrāvikā were allowed to *Saṁgha* in ancient India. Jaina Śrāvikās were allowed to read Jaina Scriptures. *Śrāvaka* is not possible without *Mūla Guṇa* or *Mukhya Guṇa. Mūla* is the name of the root. As tree cannot survive without root so also one cannot become *Śrāvaka* without *Mūla Guṇa* or *Mukhya Guṇa.*

Main Principles

The main principles of *Śrāvaka Dharma* are not rigid but simple to be followed. Some times there are same principles emphasized by different authors in their works. These principles are as follows:

Mūla Guṇa : *Mūla Guṇas* as divided into *Mūla Guṇa Gati* and *Mūla Guṇa Dhārī,* together they are called *Aṣṭa Mūla Guṇa.*

Aṣṭa Mūla Guṇa : Abstinence from wine, meat, honey and five *Udumbar* fruits are *Aṣṭa Mūla Guṇa.*

Giving up of seven vices is the primarily duty of *Śrāvaka.* Seven Vices (*Sapta Vyasanas*) are as follows : (1) Gambling, (2) Meat, (3) Wine, (4) Prostitution, (5) Stealing, (6) Relation with other women (7) Hunting.

Five great Sins : (1) Violence, (2) Untruthfulness, (3) Stealing, (4) No celibacy, and (5) Possessions.

Other Mūla Guṇas : No food after sunset, avoiding unfiltered water and inedible food. These are *Mūla Guṇa Tyāgī* because people abstained from these vices.

There are also *Aṣṭa Mūla Guṇa Dhārī*. There were so called because they followed *Mūla Guṇas Dhārī*. They are as follows:

(1) Self- study, (2) Self-restrain, (3) Worship of Deva *Guru* and religious works, (4) Kindness to living beings.

Principles of Śrāvaka religion are distinct from other religions as it is based on ethics and not on rituals. It influences the large masses and continued to survive for long time. They were liberal in their attitude because they did not propagate religious fanaticism. They believed in religious tolerationand equality and thus influenced other religions. This religion improved the family life and also rendered great service to the society by promoting welfare activities. It controlled polygamy. This religion was very effective in controlling the evils during Muslim-period, It was also important form the health point of view as by eating food before sunset, drinking filtered water, fasting on certain days, people led healthy life.

Chapter 16

Conclusion

GOLDEN AGE OF VIKRAMĀDITYA

Introduction

Vikramāditya had a versatile personality and guided himself in various fields of life. His achievements in politics were great. He patronised art and literature. He had very few equals in Indian history. His personal accomplishment were many. In generosity, courage, devotion to duty, insight in human affairs and many virtues of head and heart, he was an ideal to be adored and followed *Kṛta Yuga* was used for the first time indicating Golden period.

1. **Conquest and Extent of Empire:** Vikramāditya was the great conqueror as known from the literary sources and archaeology. We know about his conquests and extent of the empire. The description of conquests in *Kathā Sarita Sāgara* is not reliable. It is known from the

history that foreigners such as Indo-Greek, Indo-Scythians, Indo-Pārthians, Śakas and Kuṣāṇas invaded the *Vikram's* kingdom. Vikramāditya defeated these foreigners and started the Vikram era in 57 B.C. and it is of great significance that this era for the first time also began to be called *Kṛta-Yuga.* Looking at the deeds, his neighbours should be included in the Golden age.

2. Special Administration : The administration of Vikramāditya was unique and ideal. There are certain circumstances which led to the changes in administration of Vikramāditya. It begin to be based on Śaka Kṣatrapa type of administration. Ujjain was the Capital. Chaṣṭana was the head of the administration. This administration was also prevalent in Śuṅga Sātavāhana period. This administration was based on the territorial and offical type of units, who carried on the administration. Urban administration was also the special feature of this period. Some times there was republic head and some time official heads. The administration was generally based on moral principles.

3. Religion : Vikramāditya was also famous for his religious policy. Vedic religion was revived. Buddhism was adopted by large number of people. Jainism become highly developed in this period. Jaina scholars like KundaKunda, Samantabhadra, Kalakāchārya etc. propagated Jainism throughout the country. It was the golden age in Jainism. Vikramāditya was himself the follower of his ancestral religion of Śaivism but he was tolerant towards other religion. Later on, he became the follower of Jainism because of the influence of the Jaina saints. Jaina scholar have written remarkable works during this period. Sivism, Vaiṣhnavism and the worship of mother goddess came into existence.

4. Art and Architecture : This age is also famous for the development of art and architecture. In Sāñchī, a large number of *stūpas*, monasteries and sculptures were constructed. In Ujjain also the remains of Buddhism have been found. Buddhist circular temples of this period, is well known at Bairotha. The remains of Vaiṣṇava religion have been found. The pillar of Heoliodores, temple and images has been discovered and they are important from the archaeological point of view. The temple of Nārāyaṇa Vitika at Nagari is also famous. Mathurā became a great centre of Jaina art and culture. Large number of artisans accepted Jainism. Thus, we notice unique monuments of this period. It is influenced by Greek art and then it was known by Gandhāra arts.

5. Social Conditions : The ageVikramāditya was important from the point of revolutionary social changes. Old caste disappeared and new caste was formed. Foreigners like Yavan, Śakas and Kuṣāṇas etc. were merged into Hindu society. New social works were written to meet social changes. The whole society changed and new society came into existence. Inter caste marriage also started. Food and drink habits changed. Wild tribes were converted into caste.

Republics gradually disappeared and new structures of social groups were established.

6. Economic Conditions : This age is also important from economic point of view. The kingdom of Vikramāditya established during this period, gradually became rich. A large number of coins of different types have been discovered. This shows the prosperity of the region. Because of convenient communication, trade and commerce developed. Trade with foreign countries also started. Merchants occupied important position because of their wealth. Economically, this region became prosperous. Agriculture production increased and mines were noticed. In this way the economic progress led to the golden age.

7. Education, Literature and Science : Education, literature and sciences developed exceedingly as known from different branches of knowledge.

From the Mahābhārata, it is known that Ujjain became a great seat of learning because of the existence of the *āśrama* of Sāndīpani in the second century B.C. It was founded by the ancient Risi Sandipani who was the tutor of Śrīkṛṣīna and Balarāma. Such was the name and fame of this institution that students from distant places came for higher studies. Some *Purāṇas* and other literary works also describe the ancient educational institution of Ujjain. Kālidāsa refers to the *Gurukulas* of Kāṇva, Vaśiṣtha, Maricha and Chyavana.

Besides the great scientist like Varāhamihira and

Āryabhaṭṭa also flourished here.[1]

They believed in the goodness in animated and animal world. All these factors prove that there was real golden age. During the age of Vikramāditya it seems that there were perfection and people followed such local traditions.

From different souces it is known that several centres of art and architecture, religion, trade and commerce and coins were found. This indicated that Malwa was very rich. From the religious centres we know that there was toleration. Thus, people became rich from different angles and so it is called the golden age.

REFERENCE

1. *Madhya Pradesh through the Ages*, p. 293.

Bibliography

1. *Archaeological Survey of India Reports,* Alexander Cunnigham.
2. *A Catalogue of the Indian coins in the British Museum,* P.C. VI.
3. Cunnigham, A., *Coins of Ancient India.*
4. *A Catalogue of the Indian Coins in the British Museum,* P.C. XXV.
5. *Annals of the Bhandarkar Oriental Research Institute,* Poona.
6. *Ancient Cities and Towns of Rajasthan,* Delhi, 1972.
7. A Catalogue of the coins in the Indian Museum, V.A. Smith, Calcutta, 1906.
8. *Buddhist India,* Prof. Rhys David.
9. *Corpus Inscriptionum Indicoroum.*
10. *Cultural Heritage of Madhya Bharat,* D.R. Patil.
11. *Catalogue of the Coins of the Nāga kings of Padāmavatī,* Gwalior, 1957.
12. Trivedi, H.V., *Indian Archaeology,* A review, Delhi.
13. *Epigraphia Indica* XXVII.
14, *Journal of the Numismatic Society of India.*
15. *Journal of the Royal Asiatic Society of Great Britain and Ireland,* London.
16. *Jainism in Rajasthan,* Sholapur, 1963.
17. *Jaina Dharma Kā Itihāsa,* Delhi, 2005.
18. *Kālidāsa and his Times,* Delhi, 1974.

19. *Lord Mahāvīra and his Times*, Delhi, 1974.
20. *Malwa through the Ages*, Delhi, 1972.
21. *Madhya Pradesh through the Ages*, Delhi, 1997.
22. *Madhya Kālīnā Malwa Mein Jaina Dharma*, 1993.
23. *Malwa Añchal Kā Jaina Dharma Kā Itihās and Abhilokhāya Srota*, Ujjain, 2002.
24. *Malwa Ānchal Kā Jaina Lekha*, Ujjain, 1995.
25. *Pre-History and Proto-History of India*, Delhi, 1979.
26. *Select inscriptions bearing on Indian History and Civilization*, Volume I, Calcutta, 1965.
27. Vikramāditya of Ujjaiyinī.
28. *Vikrama Volume*.

INDEX

G

H

I

J

K

PLATES

Pl. 1 : General View of the pillar of heliodoris

Pl. 2 : General view of Sanchi Stupa, Sanchi

Pl. 3 : Front face of northern Gateway, Sanchi Stupa 1, Sanchi

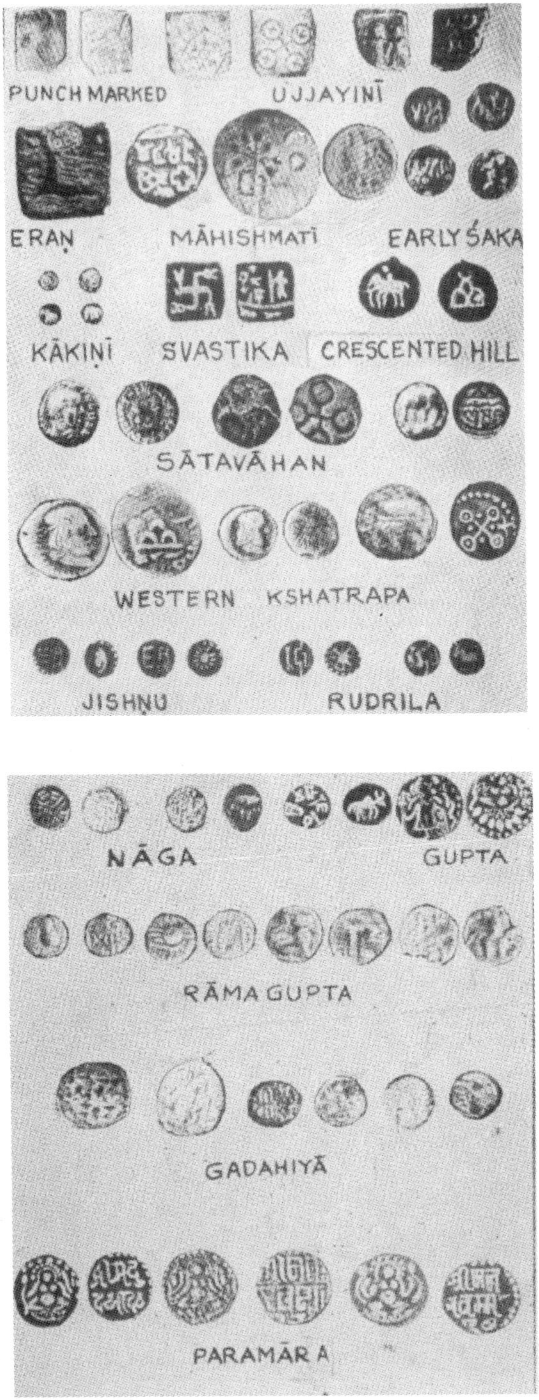

Pl. 4 : Ancient coins of malwa

Pl. 5(a) : Copper Coins of Malwa

Pl. 5 (b) : Coins of Parmaras, Malwa

Pl. 6 : Ujjaini Coins

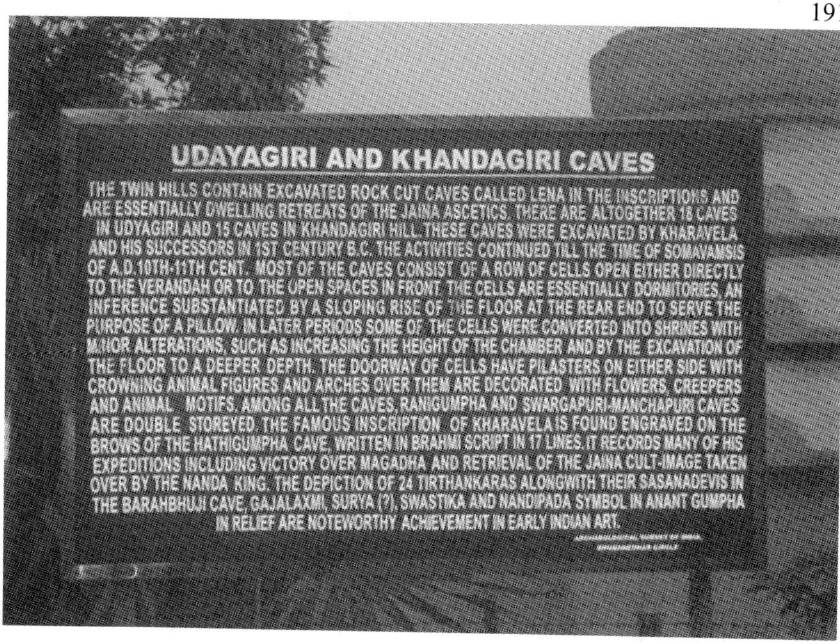

Pl. 7 : Kharavela Jaina Inscriptions

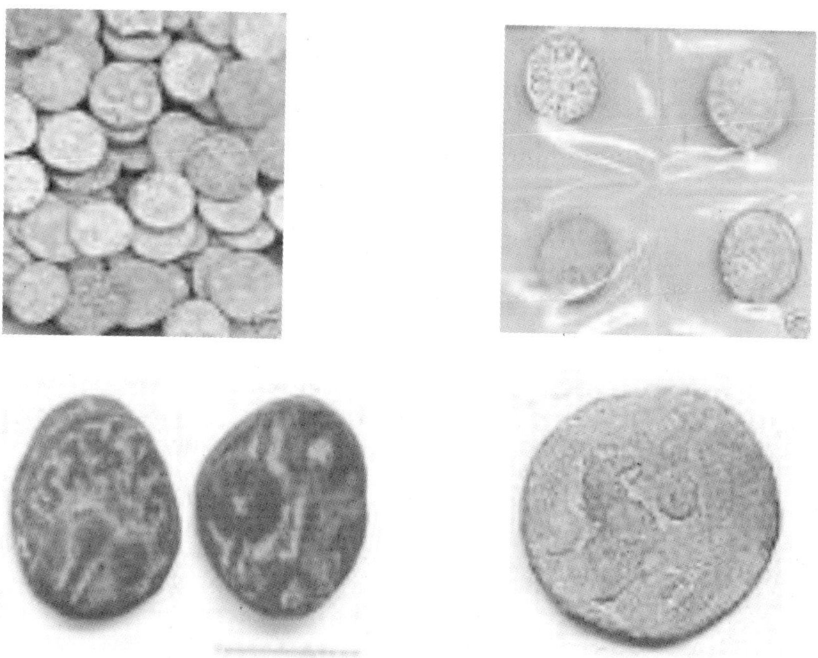

Pl. 8 : Coins of Andhra Dynasty

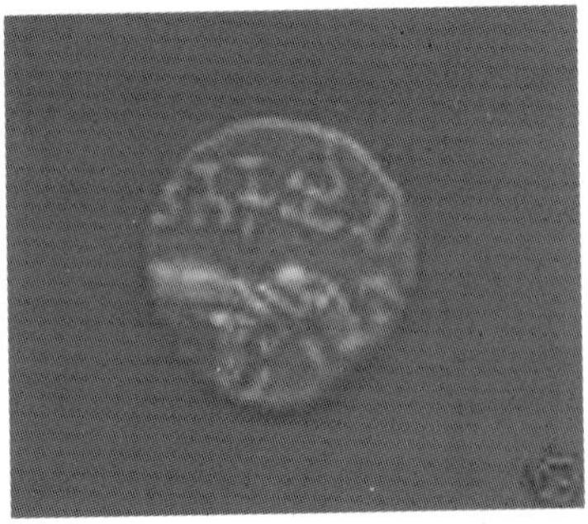

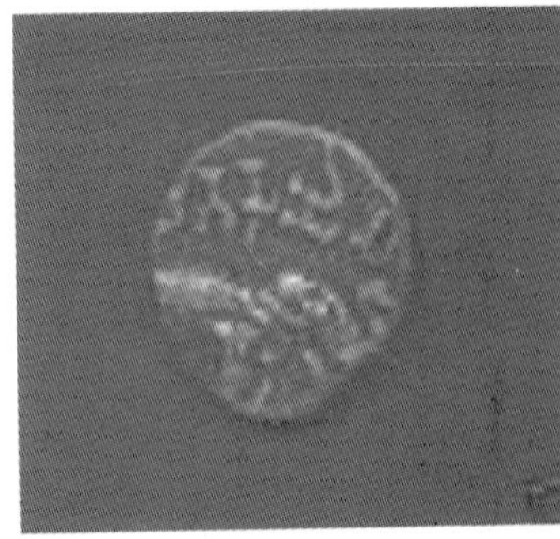

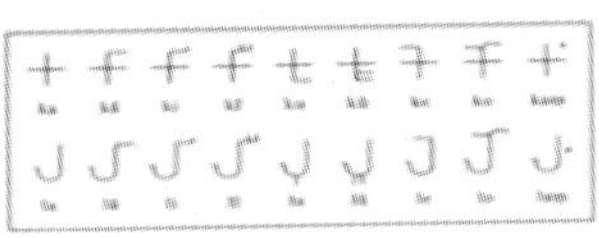

Pl. 9 : Coins of Satvahana Dynasty

Pl. 10 : Vardhamana Kushana Period

Pl. 11 : Rishabha Kushana Period

Pl. 12 : Sarasvati Goddess of Vishnu, Kushana Period

Pl. 13 : Sarasvati the wife of Brahma, Kushana Period

Pl. 14 : Lion Symbol of Ashoka Period